AMERICAN
WAR LIBRARY

★ ★ ★ ★

★ World War I ★

WEAPONS OF WAR

by Gail B. Stewart

Lucent Books, P.O. Box 289011, San Diego, CA 92198-9011

Titles in The American War Library series include:

World War II
Hitler and the Nazis
Kamikazes
Leaders and Generals
Life as a POW
Life of an American Soldier in
  Europe
Strategic Battles in Europe
Strategic Battles in the Pacific
The War at Home
Weapons of War

The Civil War
Leaders of the North and South
Life Among the Soldiers and
  Cavalry
Lincoln and the Abolition of
  Slavery
Strategic Battles
Weapons of War

Library of Congress Cataloging-in-Publication Data

Stewart, Gail B., 1949–
  Weapons of war / by Gail B. Stewart.
    p. cm. — (American war library. World War I)
Includes bibliographical references and index.
  ISBN 1-56006-837-X
  1. World War, 1914–1918—Juvenile literature. 2. World War,
1914–1918—Equipment and supplies—Juvenile literature. 3. Military
weapons—History—20th century—Juvenile literature. [1. World War,
1914–1918. 2. World War, 1914–1918—Equipment and supplies.
3. Military weapons—History—20th century.] I. Title. II. Series.
  D522.7 .S78 2002
  940.4'1028—dc21

                                        2001002019

Copyright 2002 by Lucent Books, Inc.
P.O. Box 289011, San Diego, California 92198-9011

Printed in the U.S.A.

★ Contents ★

A Nation Forged by War

The United States, like many nations, was forged and defined by war. Despite Benjamin Franklin's opinion that "There never was a good war or a bad peace," the United States owes its very existence to the War of Independence, one to which Franklin wholeheartedly subscribed. The country forged by war in 1776 was tempered and made stronger by the Civil War in the 1860s.

The Texas Revolution, the Mexican-American War, and the Spanish-American War expanded the country's borders and gave it overseas possessions. These wars made the United States a world power, but this status came with a price, as the nation became a key but reluctant player in both World War I and World War II.

Each successive war further defined the country's role on the world stage. Following World War II, U.S. foreign policy redefined itself to focus on the role of defender, not only of the freedom of its own citizens, but also of the freedom of people everywhere. During the cold war that followed World War II until the collapse of the Soviet Union, defending the world meant fighting communism. This goal, manifested in the Korean and Vietnam conflicts, proved elusive, and soured the American public on its achievability. As the United States emerged as the world's sole superpower, American foreign policy has been guided less by national interest and more on protecting international human rights. But as involvement in Somalia and Kosovo prove, this goal has been equally elusive.

As a result, the country's view of itself changed. Bolstered by victories in World Wars I and II, Americans first relished the role of protector. But, as war followed war in a seemingly endless procession, Americans began to doubt their leaders, their motives, and themselves. The Vietnam War especially caused people to question the validity of sending its young people to die in places where they were not particularly wanted and for people who did not seem especially grateful.

While the most obvious changes brought about by America's wars have been geopolitical in nature, many other aspects of society have been touched. War often does not bring about change directly, but acts instead like the catalyst in a chemical reaction, accelerating changes already in progress.

Some of these changes have been societal. The role of women in the United States had been slowly changing, but World War II put thousands into the workforce and into uniform. They might have gone back to being housewives after the war, but equality, once experienced, would not be forgotten.

Likewise, wars have accelerated technological change. The necessity for faster airplanes and a more destructive bomb led to the development of jet planes and nuclear energy. Artificial fibers developed for parachutes in the 1940s were used in the clothing of the 1950s.

Lucent Books' American War Library covers key wars in the development of the nation. Each war is covered in several volumes, to allow for more detail, context, and to provide volumes on often neglected subjects, such as the kamikazes of World War II, or weapons used in the Civil War. As with all Lucent Books, notes, annotated bibliographies, and appendixes such as glossaries give students a launching point for further research. In addition, sidebars and archival photographs enhance the text. Together, each volume in The American War Library will aid students in understanding how America's wars have shaped and changed its politics, economics, and society.

A Bloody Transition

There was tension in the air long before the beginning of the First World War. By the spring of 1914, a nervous U.S. emissary in Germany wrote to President Woodrow Wilson that war seemed inevitable. Germany seemed to him to be on the brink of war, as did other nations of Europe. "Everybody's nerves are tense," he wrote. "It only requires a spark to set the whole thing off."[1]

Competition and Revenge

The tension had no single source. Some of it was brought on by internal unrest, as was the case in Russia. The tyranny and brutality of the czars had created a nation of people who were angry and resentful of their government. Although Russia's industries had prospered, the country was rocked by strikes and political violence, with as many as a million people taking part at a time.

Some of the tension was brought on by old grudges, as in the case of France and Germany. Back in 1871, Germany had crushed France in what came to be known as the "Lightning War" because of the speed of the conquest. In addition to paying war debts to Germany, France was forced to give up two valuable provinces along its northeast border, Alsace and Lorraine.

The loss of Alsace and Lorraine was humiliating to France; open hostility toward Germany remained more than thirty years later. One French patriot urged his countrymen not to forget the loss: "Think of it always," he advised sternly. "Speak of it never."[2]

Arms Races

In following that advice, France worked to prepare itself for a future conflict—one in which Alsace and Lorraine would be successfully brought back within its borders. In addition to stepping up the production of weapons in its factories, the French military took steps to improve its system of conscription, the process of calling large numbers of men into the army when necessary.

German troops seize a village in France's Alsace province. The loss of Alsace was humiliating to France and caused open hostility toward Germany.

As France continued its arms buildup, Germany followed—unwilling to lose its dominant status. With more natural resources than France, as well as the largest standing army in Europe, the Germans by the early 1900s had achieved amazing results. According to one historian, Germany had become "the most explosive military machine in the world . . . [with] the most productive steel mills, the best chemists, the most powerful engineering industry."[3]

Germany was competing with Britain as well as with France. Britain, which had the most skilled and well-equipped navy, had never had reason to worry about its power and status. In fact, in the early twentieth cen-

tury, one-fourth of the planet was ruled by the British Empire—proof of the nation's aggressive colonization around the world.

Although Germany could not match the British in its number of colonial holdings, it could certainly aim for naval superiority. Kaiser Wilhelm, a leader intent on establishing Germany as a world power, ordered the German fleet to double its size. When the British introduced a new type of battleship, the kaiser demanded that the Germans get it too.

A System of Alliances

As the arms race continued, the system of alliances among the European nations became more important. The major nations formed agreements with one another, one nation promising to come to the other's aid if attacked or threatened. By 1914, Europe had split into two rival camps.

France, Russia, and Britain, known as the Allies, had formed an alliance primarily because they feared powerful Germany. Nervously noting that it was sandwiched between the Allied nations of France and Russia, Germany was eager to strengthen its own alliance with Austria-Hungary. Together, these two large nations were known as the Central Powers.

The idea of the alliances was to avert war. Knowing that to attack one nation was to attack an alliance of nations would presumably keep the powers of Europe from letting a minor quarrel become something much more serious. Ironically, instead, the system of alliances in the summer of 1914 turned a regional dispute into the Great War, the First World War.

"An Archduke More or Less"

The spark that President Wilson's emissary had predicted would "set the whole thing off" occurred in Sarajevo, a town in the southern part of Austria-Hungary. Archduke Ferdinand and his wife, Sophie, were shot and killed as they were riding in a parade. The teenage assassin, a Serbian named Gavrilo Princip, was a member of a secret society from nearby Bosnia. By killing the heir to the throne of Austria-Hungary, Princip was protesting Austria-Hungary's takeover of Balkan lands.

The incident was a serious one, and the government of Austria-Hungary blamed Serbia. Russia, long a champion of the Slavic people, supported Serbia and mobilized some of its troops along the border it shared with Austria-Hungary. It was then, say historians, that the system of alliances forced the powers of Europe to line up—France and

The assassination of Archduke Ferdinand and his wife sparked World War I.

9

Britain with Russia, and Germany with Austria-Hungary.

Few understood why the European nations were going to war. The United States, at the beginning completely removed from the tensions and hostilities on the continent an ocean away, was baffled at what seemed to be a grand overreaction among the European powers. One newspaper noted, "To the world, or to a nation, an archduke more or less makes little difference."[4] In Europe, the confusion was just as profound. Before his nation officially entered the war, one British cabinet member mused, "Why four great powers should fight over Serbia no fellow can understand."[5]

A War of Unheard-of Proportions

Even though its causes weren't understood by most Europeans, the war did begin on July 28, 1914, and it was unlike anything anyone could have imagined. At first, the fighting was contained in a relatively small area, but the eventual size and scope of the "battlefield" was unheard-of. Over the course of the war, between 1914 and 1918, some 65 million men—from twenty-eight nations and five continents—were mobilized. Combined, these nations would spend $332 billion in their efforts to win the war.

The losses were staggering. It is estimated that of those 65 million men, half were killed, wounded, missing, or taken prisoner. An entire generation of European men was wiped out. And even though the United States did not enter the war until 1917, the fighting claimed more than 116,000 U.S. soldiers.

Homes, businesses, churches, and schools were also obliterated. Even the land itself was spoiled. Forests were burned and blasted until they were reduced to stubble. Large tracts of land were so bombarded with explosives and poisonous gases that they were—and remain today—totally unsuitable for farming.

The Frightening Array of Weapons

Historians say that one of the most important aspects of the First World War was the awesome array of weapons used by both sides. Some of these weapons, such as submarines and torpedoes, had seen limited use in earlier times but did not become a major factor in battle until 1914.

The machine gun was another weapon that came into its own during the First World War. The gun had been developed in the United States during the Civil War, but because of manufacturing difficulties, few were available to soldiers before that war ended. In the Great War, however, machine guns achieved a grisly importance no one could have predicted.

World War I marked the first appearance of several important modern weapons, notably the tank, the airplane, and poison gas. These would certainly prove useful in this war, but their success would be limited because military leaders had not had enough opportunity to understand their potential in battle.

Even though some of the weapons were not used to either army's full advantage, those that were used between 1914 and 1918 created a very different sort of war. An army's ability to drop explosives from the air—not just on military targets but on civilian populations—was new. This was a war that involved millions of civilians to an extent no one had ever imagined. "Never in history," says one historian, "had war reached so far from the battlefield. Everyone became a soldier, one way or another."[6]

Civilians were more than targets of opposing armies. They were invaluable to their own armies in this war, as the definition of *weapon* expanded. Notes one historian, World War I became a war of armies reaching back to their civilian populations, not just to draft huge numbers of soldiers "but also to enroll the talents of the scientist, the engineer, the propagandist, and—most of all—the economic and manufacturing might that ultimately and remorselessly tilted the scales."[7]

During the war, forests were bombarded until they were reduced to rubble.

"Hardly a Heroic Death to Be Had"

Thanks in part to the advent of the machine gun and new sorts of artillery, the notion of war changed in another way. The days of military offensives—at least those waged on the ground—came to an end during the First World War. No longer were galloping cavalry charges or forward onrushes of armed troops effective—or even prudent. This lesson was learned too late by military commanders who continued to fight in traditional ways. The senseless deaths of millions of men on both sides are a testament to the wide gap between technology and military strategy, especially in the first years of the war.

The First World War marked the beginning of an age in which weapons became more important than manpower. Historian Robert O'Connell notes that poison gas, machine guns, and bombs dropped from airplanes accomplished more than the bravest, most skilled soldiers could on the battlefield:

> Arms did not simply dominate, they did so in a manner which made a mockery of the warrior ethic. . . . Skill, strength, swiftness, cunning, and aggressiveness were rendered nearly irrelevant. Combatants were gassed, torpedoed, bombarded by invisible artillery, or mowed down randomly by puny-looking machine guns; there was hardly a heroic death to be had.[8]

Dead French soldiers await burial. The gap between technology and military strategy contributed to millions of deaths.

With or without heroes, the First World War proved to be war's turning point, the transition between traditional and modern warfare. As the young men of Europe marched off to war in the summer of 1914, no one knew how drastic the change would be, or how many lives would be lost because of it. Tragically, millions would die before their commanding officers would finally understand how to fight with—and more importantly, *against*—these new weapons.

Chapter 1

From Slaughter to Deadlock

One of the most shocking realizations of the war was how ineffective many of the existing weapons were. Both sides had devised strategies that were based in part on their use of the cavalry and other traditional weapons, such as rifles, bayonets, and light artillery. Within a very short time, however, it became clear that even though many of these traditional weapons had been modernized and improved, they were still hopelessly inadequate in this new kind of war.

But at the onset of World War I, each side believed it could win quickly. German soldiers boarding troop transport trains late that summer promised their families they'd be home before the leaves dropped from the trees. The armies of the Allies were equally optimistic—few believed the war could amount to more than a battle or two. As one Irish member of the British army later recalled, "Going to war seemed like a light-hearted business. As for the Germans, a dose of that rapid fire of ours, followed by an Irish bayonet charge, would soon fix things."[9]

Two Plans

A good part of the confidence each army felt was due to the fact that both the Central Powers and the Allies had developed war plans—specific, detailed agendas of how they could win the war in the shortest amount of time. The Schlieffen Plan, named after the former German chief of staff who created it, was developed ten years before the war began. Schlieffen was certain that because of the alliance between Russia and France, Germany would eventually have to fight a war on two fronts—east and west.

His plan set a timetable for that two-fronted war. The Schlieffen Plan called for three-fourths of the German army to storm through neutral Belgium to Paris. The other fourth of the army would be with the Austrians, holding off the Russian army. Because of Russia's size and more primitive railway system, Schlieffen estimated that the Russians would not be at full strength for six weeks. During that time, Paris would be seized, France would be demoralized, and the victorious German army would turn its attention completely to conquering the Russians on the eastern front. As the approving German kaiser predicted, "Paris for lunch, dinner in St. Petersburg."[10]

The French, too, had developed a winning formula—Plan 17. Less detailed than the Schlieffen Plan, Plan 17 was rooted in retribution and revenge for the loss of Alsace and Lorraine. It stressed the need to march straight at the center of the German army and always look to attack. Like the German plan, Plan 17 stressed offensive warfare, with an emphasis on morale and courage.

Young French officers were schooled in such warfare. They were told that, "For the attack, only two things are necessary: to know where the enemy is and to decide what to do. What the enemy intends to do is of no consequence." The key, according to the plan, was to make sure that every soldier "ardently desire the assault by bayonet as the supreme means of imposing his will upon the enemy and gaining victory."[11]

It was with this aggressive, attack-oriented view of warfare in mind that the French (soon to be joined by the British) readied themselves for battle with the Germans on the western front. The military commanders of the Allies were confident that their soldiers, whose mission would be

German military strategist Alfred von Schlieffen developed a plan to fight a war on two fronts.

to subject the German army to assault by the cold steel of the bayonet, would be well equipped.

The Soldier's Mainstay

The mainstays of the offensive war were charges by the rifle-bearing infantry and some battering by the artillery—the large guns operated by several soldiers. Traditionally, once the enemy lines had been penetrated by both the infantry charge and the artillery, the cavalry would attack.

Since the days of the first muskets, a soldier's most important weapon had always been the side arm, and this war was no different. The rifle had gone through important changes over the previous half-century, and the result was a weapon that could be loaded and fired more quickly than ever before.

Like those rifles that had been considered modern during the American Civil War, these were breechloaders—loaded easily and quickly from the back of the gun rather than the muzzle. Unlike the earlier breechloaders, however, which could be loaded with only one cartridge at a time, a soldier using one of these new rifles could slip in a clip containing several cartridges. After shooting, the soldier moved a bolt on the top of the gun, which extracted the empty cartridge case and automatically allowed a fresh one to drop into the chamber.

The French and Russian armies had adequate bolt-action rifles; however, it was the British-made Lee-Enfield (usually referred to as the SMLE, for small magazine Lee-Enfield) that was widely considered the best bolt-action rifle of its time. The SMLE used a ten-cartridge clip rather than the three- or five-cartridge clips of other bolt-action rifles. With the SMLE, an expert marksman could fire as many as fifteen rounds in a minute, almost unheard of in 1914. Because of the gun's relatively short barrel, cavalry troops found it easy to handle from the back of a horse.

"It Was All So Easy"

An almost legendary display with the SMLE occurred early in the war at Mons. The British Expeditionary Force (BEF), the all-professional army that came to France in August 1914, had trained extensively with the SMLE. Any of the men could produce fifteen well-aimed shots in a minute; many of them could produce twice that many.

Having taken cover along a canal, the British troops found themselves being attacked by a much larger German army. With no artillery and only two machine

Lee-Enfield rifles such as these were capable of firing fifteen rounds in a minute.

guns, the BEF used their skill with the rifles to hold back the Germans. So rapid was their fire, in fact, that afterward, German officers informed their commanders that the BEF had all been using machine guns against them.

One British corporal recalled how easy it was shooting with the rifle as the tightly packed German regiments came at them. "Our rapid fire was appalling," he marveled. "And the worst marksman could not miss. . . . It was all so easy."[12]

In his journal, another British soldier indicated that he, too, found that with his rifle, defending his position was almost effortless:

> Bloody Hell! You couldn't see the earth for them there were that many. Time after time they gave the order "Rapid Fire." Well, you didn't wait for the order, really! You'd see a lot of them coming in a mass on the other side of the canal, and you just let them have it. They kept retreating, and then coming forward, and then retreating again. . . . I don't know how many saw them off.[13]

The Offensive Artillery

Like the rifle, the field guns of the artillery had also undergone improvements in the years leading up to the war. They could be breech-loaded, and since the charge of gunpowder was contained in the shell rather than added separately, artillery pieces could be loaded more quickly. The most important improvement, however, was eliminating a troublesome aspect of field guns—the recoil.

The large explosion that occurred when an artillery gun was fired caused it to lurch backwards, often five feet or more. Not only did the recoil result in injuries to the artillery crew, it wasted valuable time. Each time the gun was fired, it had to be relaid so that it was in the properly aimed position to fire again. For that reason, artillery pieces could almost never be fired faster than five or six times in a minute.

The French were the first to solve the problem, and the resulting gun, known as "the 75" (because of its .75-millimeter bore), was considered the finest artillery piece in the world. To do away with recoil, the gun's creators set it on a cradle. When it was fired, it slid back along the cradle and the recoil was taken up by a hydraulic buffer—similar to an automobile's shock absorber. The gun would then slide back into position, ready to be loaded and fired again in a very short time.

The 75, as well as the guns modeled after it, was able to fire between fifteen and twenty rounds a minute with relatively high accuracy. Against the German army caught in the open, it was especially lethal. Early in the war, a tightly bunched formation of the German army intending to invade the town of Nancy first marched toward the French infantry, then fled to the shelter of a forest. As a war correspondent for the *London Times* looked on, a French artillery battalion of 75s opened fire:

At some places at [the forest's] base, the bodies were piled up five or six feet high, and when the survivors took cover behind the heaps of dead and wounded, the 75s still raked them through and through, smothering dead and living in a horrible mire of flesh and blood, while the 75s, firing over the heads of the front ranks, finished off the work further back. The losses were enormous. Thousands of German dead were left lying on the plain, and in the evening they asked and were granted a few hours' truce to bury them."[14]

"Thank God We Don't Have Any!"

The French army was pleased with the 75's light weight and mobility—just the right thing, they thought, for a quick, offensive war. In fact, one staff officer who was questioned about the army's lack of heavy artillery is said to have replied, "Thank God we don't have any! What gives the French army its force is the lightness of its cannon."[15]

The French and other Allies depended so much on that gun that they failed to build

French soldiers stand next to a 75, a weapon that was lethal against the German army.

Beyond the Limits of Human Endurance

In his book *Great Weapons of World War I*, William G. Dooly Jr. quotes a *London Times* war correspondent named Gerald Campbell who wrote extensively about the experience of the infantry and artillery batteries of the war. The following excerpt is Campbell's attempt to convey the volume of the artillery pieces used during trench warfare.

To the spectator, the noise is so tremendous that it seems that it must be beyond the limits of human endurance to face the storm of steel and fire. At the hottest moments it keeps changing curiously and horribly in character, volume, and tempo, rising and falling with alternating diminuendo and crescendo and hurrying and slackening pace. It is all extraordinarily relentless.

Sometimes the deafening volley of reports sound like a clattering of a clumsy, lumbering wagon, jolting heavily over the frozen ruts of a rough country lane; sometimes like the brisk hammering of thousands of carpenters and riveters at work on thousands of heavy goods on trains thundering and bumping over uneven points and meeting every now and then in hideous collision.

[Yet they are distinguishable]. . . the heavy slow boom of the big guns, the vicious sharp bang of the field pieces, with their lightning-like velocity and shattering irresistible force, the shriek of the shells . . . and most awful of all, I think, the sudden unexpected silences, which make you hold your breath and wait—like a condemned murderer with the noose around his neck must wait on the scaffold—for the dreaded moment which you know will come when the storm will begin all over again.

heavier artillery. When the war began, in addition to twenty-eight hundred 75s, the French had only two hundred heavy pieces—the large guns that could decimate targets much farther away. The British army was also low on heavy artillery, as was the United States when it entered the war in 1917.

The German army was far more prepared; in 1914, it had about eighty-two hundred pieces of artillery, thousands more than the Allies' armies put together. Some of these German guns were powerful enough to send shells more than twice as far as the 75 could, as British troops found in August 1914 near Mons.

The British light artillery was called on to open fire, but the shells fell far short of the German line. As one British general later recalled, "I turned to the battery commander and said sharply, 'For God's sake, hit them!' It was Foreman—a splendid officer—but his reply was dampening; 'I cannot get another yard of these guns.'" The German heavy artillery had no such trouble. "It was not many minutes," the general said, "before the German shells were pitching among us in reply to our fire."[16]

Even though the Allies could not compete with the German artillery in distance, they were not concerned in the early stages of the war. Plan 17 called for attacking; therefore, they would continue to rely on weapons that were light and easy to move.

The Most Lethal Weapon

While there was no doubt that the rifle and light auxiliary had improved by the onset of the war, there was one weapon in the Allies' arsenal that had become more lethal than any other—the machine gun. One of the earliest models of the machine gun, the Gatling gun, had made a very brief appearance in the American Civil War, but it could not be developed and produced in time to be battle-tested before the war ended in 1865. In the First World War, however, the machine gun was such a factor that one historian says that the name of the man who perfected it "is more deeply engraved on the real history of the World War than that of any other man."[17]

Those who tested the machine gun shortly after the Civil War found several problems with it. They complained about how heavy and cumbersome it was. The gun also had a tendency to overheat; when this occurred, the only remedy was to let it sit for several minutes. Finally, the early machine gun was difficult to use since it had to be cranked by hand.

Even though the weapon received such poor reviews in 1865, the idea of a gun that could fire more than 120 shots per minute was too appealing to forget about. If its problems could be fixed, many soldiers believed, the machine gun could be extremely effective. Because of its possibilities in future wars, several inventors tried their hand at perfecting the machine gun.

Hiram Maxim, an inventor from Maine, succeeded. A friend had told Maxim in 1882 that if he wanted to make a fortune, he should invent a great new weapon for the Europeans to use on one another because he believed they were going to war soon. Intrigued, Maxim focused his creative energy on making a truly automatic gun. What he came up with would be copied by every army in the world.

With Just a Finger

If the gun was to really be a machine, it had to be capable of ejecting each spent cartridge and loading in the next, rather than needing a soldier to crank it. To accomplish this, Maxim used the energy from the gun's recoil.

Hiram Maxim demonstrates his machine gun, which would be copied by every army in the world.

The ammunition—250 cartridges fitted to a belt moving from right to left—is initially loaded into the gun's breech. The first cartridge is inserted into the gun's barrel by hand, and when the trigger is pulled, the gun recoils. According to one British weapons expert, the gun does the rest:

> During the recoil, the breech is opened, the empty shell extracted, the firing pin cocked, and a cartridge brought into position and pushed into the barrel. The force of the recoil stores up energy in a spiral spring which returns the barrel to the firing position, inserts the cartridge, and closes the breech. The gun is automatically fired as long as the trigger is pulled.[18]

Not only did the gun fire automatically, it did so at astonishing speed. In addition, the gun barrel was enclosed by a thin water jacket to prevent it from overheating. At an 1889 demonstration for British officials, Maxim fired his gun accurately at a rate of six hundred shots per minute—with just the touch of a finger. The British were impressed, as were the other European military leaders who saw the gun at another demonstration soon afterward. Surprisingly, however, no country was very interested in buying the gun.

Spraying Bullets Like a Garden Hose

The reason, say historians, is that it seemed too easy a method of killing. A soldier using the Maxim gun (as it was known) did not have to possess either skill or bravery, which rankled the traditional military leadership of the time. According to that leadership, an army had to put the highest value on skill and bravery, or any victory achieved would not be honorable. In his book *Of Arms and Men*, historian Robert L. O'Connell writes that the Maxim gun, "which sprayed bullets like a garden hose sprayed water not only contradicted these values, it made a mockery of them."[19]

Even though the Maxim gun initially found little support among the military in Europe, it was embraced enthusiastically by the colonial armies of those same nations. Germany and Britain, for example, occupied nations in Asia and Africa and found Maxim's gun an easy way for a tiny minority to control a large hostile population.

There were scores of bloody instances of the gun's effectiveness. One example occurred at the turn of the century, when two Germans with two machine guns fired from inside a hut that gave them a clear line of fire against a large Tanzanian population. Within minutes, the Germans had killed more than a thousand people. A handful of English soldiers achieved an even more astonishing result in Sudan in 1896. With machine guns and a cannon, the English mowed down some twenty thousand Dervishes as they attacked on horseback, armed only with lances.

Such deadly results helped link the self-interest of European colonialists with the Maxim gun. In fact, a popular satire of the time asserted that "Whatever happens, we

Entrenched soldiers such as these German troops easily repelled strong offensive attacks with machine guns.

have got the Maxim gun, and they have not."[20]

But despite the gun's lethal track record, the Allies were reluctant to purchase it for the First World War. Britain, for example, had only two machine guns per battalion when the war began; the BEF was unsure of how to use the gun as an offensive weapon. The British version of the Maxim, the Vickers gun, was a source of confusion for the army; military leaders couldn't agree on whether it should be used as an artillery piece or as part of the infantry. As late as 1915, Sir Douglas Haig, the commander of the British army, insisted, "The machine gun is a much-overrated weapon, and two per battalion is more than sufficient."[21]

Digging In

Yet as the war continued, it became apparent that the best new weapons of the infantry and artillery were defensive, not offensive. Few, if any, successful attacks against German troops were accomplished by Allied soldiers brandishing rifles, light artillery such as the 75, or machine guns. On the other hand, every time either army attempted a strong attack against entrenched troops, it was quickly and cruelly repelled by these same weapons.

For this reason, the war of movement, during which the Germans were attempting to reach Paris, did not last long. By the autumn of 1914, the French and British armies had stopped the Germans just short of the city, driving them backward from the river Marne to the river Aisne. After that battle, known as the Battle of the Marne, both armies dug in, taking a defensive (and much safer) posture, relying on their machine guns and artillery to repel any attack. They dug shallow trenches, just deep enough to supply a little protection from enemy machine-gun fire.

Both armies made attempts to spread out, hoping to outflank each other, but were unsuccessful. As these troops were stymied, they too would dig trenches. By Christmas 1914, two parallel lines of entrenched armies had been dug through France for some 460 miles, from Switzerland to the English Channel. The quick, offensive war of the Schlieffen Plan and Plan 17 had been paralyzed by the very weapons that were supposed to help them succeed.

Digging the Perfect System

The hastily dug trenches that Allied soldiers had first used to give their gunners a spot to make a defensive stand in battle were hardly suitable for lengthy stays. As the weeks went on, soldiers worked with spade and shovel to construct deeper trenches that would provide more protection from artillery shells and machine-gun fire. These deep, intricately designed trench systems became weapons in themselves, and called for a whole new type of

warfare than what had been used up till that point.

The Allies' trench line was actually three lines. The one closest to the enemy's trench was the front line; behind it were two "support" trenches, where men and supplies were on hand. Underground communications trenches spiderwebbed throughout the trench system, allowing men, supplies, and ammunition to be moved as necessary.

Although the initial foxholes were only a foot or two deep, the trench system of the Allies was between seven and eight feet deep, so soldiers could move about without worrying about getting shot. The trenches also contained steps from which soldiers could fire or quickly observe the enemy. The trenches were zigzagged as well; otherwise, if an enemy soldier with a machine gun somehow got into an Allied trench, he could easily kill everyone in it by firing down its length.

No-Man's-Land

The frontline trenches of the two armies were often two hundred or three hundred yards apart; however, in some cases, there was a distance of only twenty-five yards between them. It was crucial for the Allies to ensure that their trenches were safe from an offensive attack. As both armies knew, the only route such an attack could take would be across that desolate strip of land between the two armies known as no-man's-land.

Of course, machine-gun posts set up in the trenches were always manned, and any available artillery was positioned behind the third trench in case of an attack. Soldiers in the trenches had their rifles, too. Any massed offensive movement would have a great deal of difficulty succeeding against these weapons.

However, at night, when there was almost no visibility, the threat of a secret raid was unsettling. It was to prevent such an attack that one of trench warfare's most visible weapons was used. Coiled barbed wire was an American invention, intended as a way of keeping large herds of cattle enclosed on the prairie. Its purposes in war would be far more sinister.

Barbed Wire

What makes barbed wire so effective are the thorny projections which can grab—and hold—clothing or skin. Because of this, both armies used thousands of miles of barbed wire to create entanglements in front of their trenches. Wiring parties constructed and repaired entanglements, one of the most detested and feared of all trench duties.

The soldiers of the wiring party carried large metal pickets six or seven feet long.

Allied soldiers constructed deep trenches to protect themselves from artillery shells and machine-gun fire.

The pickets were set into the ground and hammered, with sandbags wrapped around the hammer to muffle the noise. After the pickets were firmly in place, the soldiers unrolled long lengths of coiled barbed wire and fastened it to the pickets. Sometimes tin

"Our Army Is Drowning in Its Own Blood"

Since the Allies and the Central Powers had both counted on winning the war quickly, they were unprepared for the kind of war that actually resulted. Both sides were low on artillery shells and guns, rifle ammunition, and other necessities. However, no army was as woefully underprepared as the Russian army.

Shortages of basics such as rifles and bullets contributed to the collapse of the Russian armies on the eastern front of the war. During the spring and summer of 1915, Russia lost more than 1 million soldiers. German soldiers returned home telling stories of Russian soldiers armed with rocks or clubs.

Russian factories could turn out only fifty thousand rifles per month. But Russian military leaders needed 1.5 million just to arm those soldiers already at the front. The Russian chief of staff, General Bielaiev, painted a grim picture for the French ambassador, quoted in William G. Dooly's *Great Weapons of World War I.*

In several infantry regiments which have taken part in the recent battles at least one-third of the men had no rifle. These poor devils had to wait patiently under a shower of shrapnel until their comrades fell before their eyes and they could pick up their arms. . . . It is quite true that our [peasants] have an amazing capacity for endurance and resignation, but that doesn't make it any less ghastly. . . . Today, with its artillery and infantry dumb [mute], our army is drowning in its own blood.

cans were attached as a makeshift alarm that would alert the soldiers if someone attempted to get through the wire.

It was important for the allies to set up the barbed wire as far away from their own frontline trench as possible; otherwise, a German soldier might be able to get close enough to throw a grenade, killing a large number of people. Sometimes breaks in the entanglements were made to lure a soldier into an area monitored by a sniper or machine gunner.

Barbed wire proved to be almost impossible to escape from, as many Allied soldiers learned firsthand from the wire strung in front of German trenches. In a letter home, one private wrote of the sadness and frustration of seeing someone he knew trapped in no-man's-land on barbed wire:

There is one of our officers hanging on the German barbed wire and a lot of attempts have been made to get him, and a lot of brave men have lost their lives in the attempt. The Germans know that we are sure to try and get him in so all they have to do is to put two or three fixed rifles on to him and fire every few seconds—he must be riddled with bullets by now."[22]

Grenades

The proximity of the two sides' trenches made the grenade a useful weapon, too. Grenades were not new; forms of these hand-held bombs had been used in siege warfare for centuries. The basic design had

A soldier tosses a "Grenade No. 1," a crucial weapon in trench warfare.

always been simple: a metal container—usually round, about the same size as a small cannonball—filled with gunpowder or other explosive, and with a slow-burning fuse. After lighting the grenade, a soldier would throw it into an enemy soldiers' position, where it would quickly explode.

Because warfare in the past two centuries had become more offense-minded, the grenade had evolved very little. They were heavy and cumbersome, exceedingly difficult for even a strong man to throw thirty or forty yards—hardly useful in an at-

tacking war. Some grenades were the traditional cannonball shape; others, like the British "Grenade No. 1," had an eighteen-inch wooden handle the soldier hung onto when hurling it, as well as streamers to make it land nose first. Although the No. 1 grenades were a bit easier to launch than other types, their fuses were often temperamental, allowing the spark to go out suddenly.

As the soldiers in the autumn of 1914 took to the trenches, it was clear that the grenade could be a crucial weapon, especially in situations where the trenches were close together. A well-placed grenade could clear out an enemy lookout post or machine-gun nest. It could be used against an enemy assault, especially one that was being slowed by barbed wire.

Yet neither type of grenade was available to the Allied soldiers. Those who had overseen the military buildup before the war had not even considered that grenades would be useful. As a result, soldiers were reduced to fashioning their own grenades while waiting for munitions factories back home to ship real ones. Some men filled empty fruit or jam cans with explosives and experimented with different types of cotton for fuses. Other soldiers were more creative, cramming tiny pieces of tin and small stones in the cans to make the explosion even more deadly.

From the Suicide Club to the Mills Bomb

Although such makeshift models sometimes succeeded, others were unreliable—and sometimes dangerous to the men using them. One of the British army's creations, known as the Pitcher grenade, resulted in so many accidents that the bombing squads whose job it was to throw them became known as the Suicide Club.

The Pitcher grenade had a cap at the top that covered a string. When the string was pulled, the friction was suppposed to light the fuse underneath. The fuses were not always the same length, however, so the bomber never knew exactly how much time he had to get rid of the grenade. In addition, the powder tended to clump inside the grenade; when that happened, it failed to explode. One British soldier recalled an accident that happened to a member of the Suicide Club who attempted to throw several of the Pitchers in August 1915:

> "Two failed to explode," he reported. "The caps of all these bombs have been difficult to remove. Corporal Holden then took up a fourth bomb and the cap of this was even stiffer than the remainder had been. Just as he succeeded in getting the cap off and the string came away, the bomb exploded in his hand, killing him outright."[23]

The British War Department became involved in developing a safer, more reliable grenade, which was called the Mills bomb. Its firing mechanism was activated in two steps, rather than one. A well-made time fuse made the bomb less dangerous for the soldier throwing it. The Mills bomb was lighter than previous models, too, and was grooved in a bumpy, pineapple shape that was easier to grip and throw. French weapons manufacturers increased the grenade's usefulness—as well as its range—by developing one that could be launched in a rifle. Designed so that the rifle's bullet would actually discharge it from the gun, the grenade could be shot more than six hundred feet.

To their credit, munitions factories in England were quick to produce the Mills bomb. Whereas troops had been receiving 70 grenades per week in 1914, by July 1916 more than 800,000 were being shipped to the front each week. The British also supplied the grenade to other Allied forces, including the Americans.

A Powerful Array

As innovative and powerful as all of these weapons were, they virtually locked each army in place. What military leaders had thought were excellent offensive weapons turned out to be superior defensive weap-ons. And once settled into defensive postures, both armies honed their weapons of entrenchment.

Efforts by both armies to attack the enemy's trenches were unsuccessful. Even when an offensive effort pushed the other side back a few yards, it was at such a high cost of human life that the effort was meaninglesss. As months went by, soldiers at the front began to wonder if the war could be won at all—by either side.

We get a few of the Jerries [German soldiers] with a grenade, they get some of ours with a shell. A sniper on our side

Tunneling and Mining

One weapon used by both armies on the western front was "tunneling," secretly digging tunnels under no-man's-land and placing explosives under the enemy's trenches. When the explosives were detonated, a large segment of the trench would be destroyed, and in the confusion, the other army could mount an offensive. Tunneling and mining were slow, difficult tasks, as explained in the following excerpt from George Coppard's *With a Machine Gun to Cambrai: The Tale of a Young Tommy in Kitchener's Army.*

Le Touquet consisted of a number of huge mine craters, roughly between the German front and our own. In some cases, the edge of one crater overlapped that of another. Companies of Royal Engineers, composed of specially selected British coal miners, worked in shifts around the clock digging tunnels toward the German line. When a tunnel was completed after several days of sweating labor, tons of explosive charges were stacked at the end and primed ready for firing. Careful calculations were made to ensure that the center of the explosion would bang under the target area.

This was an underground battle against time, with both sides competing against each other to blast great holes through the earth above. With listening apparatus, the rival gangs could judge each other's progress, and draw conclusions. A continual contest went on. As soon as a mine was blasted, preparations for a new tunnel were started. On at least one occasion British and German miners clashed and fought underground, when the final partition of earth between them suddenly collapsed.

On the completion of one of the mines, the troops in the danger area withdrew when zero time for detonation was imminent. If the resultant crater had to be captured, an infantry storming party would be ready to rush forward and beat [the Germans] to it. Some of the craters measured over a hundred feet across the top, descending funnel-wise to a depth of at least 30 feet.

hits one of them, one of ours gets tangled and held in the wire and they finish him off with a machine gun. What the bloody hell good is this war," wondered a British soldier in 1916. "Call it even and make a day of it, I say.[24]

As the futility of offensive war became more apparent, military leaders turned to weapons designers for answers. If only they had a weapon that could change the rhythm of the war, that could get the armies out of the trenches, perhaps the conflict could be won. But what sort of weapon could it be? Was there anything powerful enough to break this stalemate on the western front?

★ Chapter 2 ★

Seeking a Way Out

Seeking a way to move the war out of the trenches led to the development of some of the most dramatic weapons of World War I. One of the most frightening of the new weapons was first used by the German army, but was quickly adopted by the Allies. Unlike the other military hardware, this new weapon was yellowish-green, silent, and only slightly heavier than the air it poisoned.

One Spring Evening

Along five miles of the front near the Belgian town of Ypres, the Germans carefully stacked cylinder cannisters of chlorine gas. It had been brought in secretly at night so as not to alert the Allied troops in their nearby trenches. On April 22, 1915, having decided that it was the day to use the weapon, German officers waited for the right conditions, a breeze blowing from behind their own line toward the Allied trenches.

Just after 5:00 P.M. a German plane flew overhead, dropping flares to signal that it was time to release the forty-five hundred cylinders of gas. As the German infantry began pounding the Allied trenches with artillery fire, other soldiers opened the mechanism to release the gas. Within five minutes, more than 168 tons of chlorine were floating in clouds toward the Allied trenches held by French and African troops.

As German officers had predicted, their new weapon confused the Allies, who were unprepared for the greenish-yellow cloud that engulfed them. Within minutes, fifteen thousand soldiers lay dead or injured from the powerful chemical. In the days that followed, Allied leaders spoke out against Germany for using gas as a weapon, using words like "diabolical" and "monstrous." One British officer accused the Germans of starting up "a devilish engine of warfare."[25]

Yet at the same time the Allies protested against the use of gas, they were urging their own munitions departments to provide them with the gas too. Very soon,

both armies were using chlorine and developing new and more powerful chemicals as weapons.

Allied soldiers continue firing their weapons as chlorine gas approaches their trench.

Dishonorable and Cowardly

The use of chemicals in war was certainly not a new concept in 1915. During the American Civil War, there had been a proposal to use chlorine gas on Confederate soldiers; however, Secretary of War Edwin Stanton had refused. One Confederate balloonist had suggested dropping poisonous chemicals down onto Northern troops, but his idea was also rejected.

Before the First World War, the main argument against using gas as a weapon was that it was considered an indecent way of waging war. For many centuries, many people had held the belief that wars should be fought with honor and dignity, with certain rules inherent to any conflict. Any weapon that would be indiscriminately harmful to soldiers and civilians alike—such as a land mine—was dishonorable and cowardly. So was any weapon that could produce prolonged suffering, and poison gas fit this category.

This is not to say, however, that poison gas had not been used. The British had experimented with forms of arsenic that could be loaded into artillery shells during the Crimean War in 1855. They had also used artillery shells filled with picric acid during the Boer War in South Africa in 1899, but with little success. The French had started fires of green, unaged wood in their 1854 colonial war in Algeria and had suffocated an entire tribe of people with the noxious smoke.

Clearly, the notions of what was right or wrong in warfare were becoming somewhat less certain by the end of the nineteenth century. In a well-attended international peace conference held in the Netherlands at the Hague in 1899, some European nations had proposed an official ban on "the use of projectiles the sole object of which is the diffusion of asphyxiating or deleterious gases."[26] Germany, France, Great Britain, and Russia had all signed the proposition.

Yet, just sixteen years later, the German army had used chlorine gas at Ypres. Germany insisted that its actions had not broken the Hague Treaty ban since the gas was not fired in shells but was merely borne on the wind. Germany also pointed a finger at the French army, which had used shells filled with tear gas (a far less deadly irritant) early in the war. The age of gas warfare, with all the help of modern technology, had arrived.

"A Most Horrible Sight"

Chlorine gas was the sole poison used at first by both armies. It was extremely toxic; when inhaled, it seared the windpipe and lungs, causing the victim to choke and cough. The trauma to the body caused the skin to turn a shiny gray-black. If enough of the gas was deeply inhaled, it caused a thick yellowish substance to be secreted in the lungs, a substance that was virtually impossible to cough up.

Soldiers died slow, agonizing deaths from chlorine gas.

In such instances, death was agonizingly slow. "I saw some hundred poor fellows laid out in the open," says one witness, "in the forecourt of a church, to give them all the air they could get, slowly drowning with water in their lungs—a most horrible sight, and the doctors quite powerless."[27]

Chlorine gas was especially effective against an entrenched enemy. Heavier than air, it sank down into the deep shelters the armies had constructed for protection against bullets and artillery shells. Running from the gas almost always produced a more severe reaction; taking faster breaths—a natural part of exertion—quickened the gas's effects on the lungs.

The Scramble for Protection

The immediate concern for the Allies was protecting their obviously unprepared soldiers from this new weapon. A few soldiers who escaped injury in the attack had backgrounds in chemistry and recognized the gas as chlorine. They informed their fellow soldiers that, in such an emergency, breathing through cloth that had been dipped in urine could filter the gas's deadly effects. The practice was certainly unpleasant, but it would have to do until suitable gas protection could be designed.

The attack at Ypres was followed by several more attacks, in which Allied soldiers had a chance to test their makeshift gas masks. As soon as they spotted the greenish-yellow cloud approaching, most of the men urinated on a cotton strip, an extra sock, or a handkerchief and tied the fabric over their noses and mouths. In addition to the smell, the homemade gas masks had another drawback in the case of multiple gas attacks, as one soldier noted in his journal:

When the alert went off you had to urinate on the cotton . . . tear pieces off to plug in your nostrils, shove the rest in your mouth and tie the lot on with the strip of lace curtain. Everyone obliged, but the gas was away to our left and we had the all-clear. However, about 15 minutes later the alert went again and as the lads had made such a good effort in the first instance, nothing was forthcoming at such short notice and it was really funny to see us all making desperate efforts."[28]

In the following months, British and French scientists worked to create more suitable gas protection. In the meantime, handkerchiefs and socks were replaced by cotton pads—sometimes women's sanitary pads—that could be strapped over the soldier's nose and mouth. The pads, which Red Cross workers turned out at the rate of 1 million per day, were dipped in a chemical solution called bicarbonate of soda to neutralize the chlorine gas. Buckets of the solution soon became a fixture in the front trench line.

"It Was a Foul Way to Kill Human Beings"

Besides developing protective gear for their soldiers in 1915, the Allied command was

Gas and the Company Animals

Even though they were officially forbidden to do so, many infantry units kept dogs and cats for company mascots, and gas units were no different. However, the poison gas was as lethal (or more so) to animals as it was to humans, as Donald Richter notes in *Chemical Soldiers: British Gas Warfare in World War I*.

A 2nd Battalion [Special Brigade] order in February 1916 directed that all dogs in possession of men in the battalion be destroyed or handed over to civilians, but group pictures of gas units with dog mascots show how little the directive was obeyed. C Company's section 14 group picture in 1917 features Marquis, the section mascot, front and center. Sadly, Marquis succumbed to gas poisoning early in 1918 when he broke loose from his chain during a practice gas discharge and ran into the cloud. K Company kept a dog named Madame Spigot.

Frequently, dogs sensed the presence of gas in the trenches before their human occupants did, their sickness providing early warning. A major with the Royal Engineers writes of a company cat that got slightly gassed in 1916 and "wheezed very much" but recovered. The effect of gas on horses was particularly tragic, and in spite of ill-fitting horse gas masks, gas "killed off the horses like flies." A lieutenant with the 5th Worcesters discovered that mules, also used extensively for transport, were terrified by the sight of anyone wearing a gas mask, and therefore prone to panic during gas attacks.

experimenting with more deadly forms of gas. One was phosgene, sometimes called "choking gas." Phosgene was eighteen times more lethal than chlorine and had two other advantages. First, unlike chlorine, which could be easily seen before its effects were felt, phosgene was invisible. Second, it had a pleasant smell, like newly cut grass.

Another asset of using phosgene as a weapon was that those who breathed it suffered only mild discomfort at first. As a result, soldiers breathed in large doses of the phosgene not realizing what horrors would occur many hours later, when the body's respiratory tract shut down and led to a slow, excrutiating death by asphyxiation. Admitted British meteorologist Dr. H. Cotton, "It was a foul way to kill human beings, but the Germans started it."[29]

When the Germans also began using phosgene, the Allies were faced with a new problem: The primitive gas protection gear that protected them from chlorine was ineffective against phosgene. Especially worrisome was the fact that artillery shells filled with the gas were being shot from great distances, leaving any soldier within artillery range vulnerable, day or night. More sophisticated gas masks were needed, and soon.

Hoods, Nose Clips, and Breathing Boxes

The answer was an apparatus that could be worn for long stretches of time whenever a gas attack seemed to be a possibility. British and French troops issued hood-shaped helmets made of flannel that could be tucked into the uniform shirt. These gas masks had celluloid goggles sewn in to protect the eyes from the burning gas. The flannel was treated with chemicals that could neutralize the gas and was kept moist with glycerine so that soldiers were not forced to keep the mask wet, as they had had to do with the cotton pads.

Various armies improved these masks over the next few years. The French found that the celluloid eyepieces had a tendency to crack, so they replaced them with glass. Glass did not crack, but it fogged up on the inside; U.S. armaments engineers solved this problem by adding an inner ring around the eyepieces that was designed to hold a little channel of water. When the wearer of the mask found the glass becoming foggy, he could clear it by shaking his head, thereby allowing the water inside to rinse the fog from the glass.

Since the early masks were loose fitting, soldiers wore nose clips to ensure that they didn't inhale any gas that got inside the mask. A mouth tube, called a hosepipe, attached to a filter of charcoal or talc and kept the air that wearers breathed gas-free.

These masks were also ideal for the horses that were depended on for hauling and moving equipment. Although their eyes were not as sensitive to gas as humans' were, hundreds of horses died by inhaling phosgene or chlorine gas every time there was a gas attack. The masks were very loose and fit over a horse's muzzle. Though the absence of nose clips meant that there was less protection than with the human ver-

sion, the masks cut down on the numbers of horses killed by gas.

By the time the United States entered the war in 1917, designers had done away with the baggy hoods and nose clips by developing tighter-fitting masks. However, the masks still relied on a hosepipe that connected to a filtered "breathing box." This lightweight box hung like a bib around a soldier's neck or, in some cases, could be clipped or strapped on his back.

Gas masks improved soldiers' chances of surviving chemical warfare in World War I.

The Undisputed King of Poison Gases

As masks became more effective, both armies worked to develop stronger gas weapons. Sometimes, they could achieve success by combining two types of gas, such as phosgene and a gas called chloropicrin, which was known to cause nausea. The chloropicrin could penetrate gas masks, and when a stricken soldier removed his mask to vomit, he would inhale the phosgene.

By the end of the war, more than fifty different chemicals were used as weapons. The most devastating was an oily brown substance first introduced by the Germans (and later produced by the Allies). Its sharp smell was a combination of horseradish and mustard, so the substance became widely known as "mustard gas."

Because the gas was not easily detected at first, soldiers were often exposed long before they felt any ill effects. Hours after exposure, the gas blistered the skin, eyes, and respiratory tract with burns so painful that victims often had to be strapped to their beds. And while gas masks could prevent internal injuries, the fumes from mustard gas could easily seep into boots and clothing, causing white-hot external burning.

One doctor vividly remembered his first experience treating men who had been exposed to mustard gas. "The men we took were covered in blisters," he wrote in his journal. "The size of your palm, most of

French soldiers attack German trenches with phosgene gas. More than one hundred thousand tons of chemicals were used during the First World War.

them. In any tender, warm place, under the arms, between the legs, and over the face and neck. All their eyes were streaming."[30]

Mustard gas was easier to use than chlorine and other cannister gas. Because so little of the concentrated substance was needed to produce the desired effect, it could be added to ammunition shells. Even if no soldiers were hit directly by the shells, the effects would be felt for a long time afterward; soil contaminated with mustard gas continued to be dangerous for weeks.

Largely Ineffective

A total of 100,000 tons of poisonous chemicals were used over four years of the war and resulted in more than 1 million casualties.

Interestingly, American soldiers suffered a higher rate of injuries from gas than other soldiers did; about 27 percent of their casualties were from gas, especially mustard gas, which was introduced at about the same time that the United States entered the war.

But as horrific as it was, gas was not as useful as military leaders had hoped. Some historians say that the Germans could have taken far more advantage of its effects at Ypres in 1915, for the Allies were totally unprepared for a gas attack. Had the Germans charged toward the Allied line as that five-mile section was in panic, they almost certainly would have made a significant gain.

Instead, the German army seemed as bewildered by the results of the gas as the Allies. Perhaps not expecting that the attack would be so successful, the German command had failed to bring more men to that part of the line. Once the element of surprise was gone, the opportunity for a decisive gain was gone, for soon afterward gas masks made armies less vulnerable. Writes weapons expert William G. Dooly Jr., "This failure to exploit their surprise key to breaking out of the trench deadlock . . . ranks as one of the more serious military blunders of World War I."[31]

Gas was an ineffective weapon for other reasons as well. It was decidedly difficult to use, for a sudden shift in the wind could send poisonous gas back into the launchers' faces. In addition, the cannisters often leaked before they could be released and filled the trench with gas. "God, what a game!" complained one angry British sol-dier at the Battle of Loos. "The rotten apparatus they had given us was leaking all over the place and we were working in a cloud of gas."[32]

The Landship

A weapon that was far more successful than gas in moving the war out of the trenches was the tank, which made its first appearance in the fall of 1916. Unlike some other new weapons, the tank was clearly designed to attack, to bridge the gap of no-man's-land between Allied and German trenches without fear of machine-gun fire from the entrenched German army.

The idea of an armored vehicle was old even at the time of the First World War; possible designs for circular, thick-walled fighting machines had been sketched by Leonardo da Vinci in the early sixteenth century. But to be armored in World War I meant having metal walls thick enough to resist rifled ammunition and grenades, and how could such a heavy vehicle be powered? Not until the internal combustion engine was invented in the early twentieth century did the idea cross into the realm of possibility.

The British had developed an armored automobile fitted with machine guns after the German invasion of France. The vehicle was designed to guard Allied airfields, but after the two armies became entrenched and the roads throughout France and Belgium were scarred with barbed wire and craters from exploded ammunition, the armored car was no longer useful.

However, a British colonel, Ernest Swinton, was convinced that combining armor with an American farm tractor with a caterpillar track would produce a useful weapon for the Allies. He suggested the idea—he called it a "landship"—to a colleague, who in turn sent a proposal to high-ranking military officials. According to the proposal, this landship "with caterpillar driving gear . . . [would be able to] run down barbed wire by sheer weight, to give some cover to men creeping up behind, and to support the advance with machine-gun fire."[33]

Swinton's ideas were not taken seriously by his superiors. Said one high-ranking official, "Caterpillar landships are idiotic and useless. Nobody has asked for them and nobody wants them." Another predicted that even with the metal plating, "the armored caterpillar would be shot up by guns."[34]

But Britain's first lord of the navy, Winston Churchill, saw a glimmer of possibility in the idea. Churchill had been looking into armored vehicles to allow naval detachments to safely cross broken ground and trench areas on the Belgian coast. If the army didn't want such a vehicle, Churchill reasoned, the navy could certainly put it to use. Early in

Tanks proved even more successful than chemical warfare in moving the war out of the trenches.

1915 Churchill gave Swinton encouragement and the permission he needed to start developing the landship.

Big Willie and Mother

Designers thought that for the weapon to be effective, it must be able to climb a vertical earth barrier five feet high and cross a trench eight feet wide. In addition, it would need to be able to achieve a top speed of four miles per hour on flat ground, while housing a crew of eight to ten to either navigate or man the guns.

It took more than a year for designers to come up with a vehicle that could do all of these things successfully. The first model, the Mark I, was produced in both "male" and "female" types. The male model was armed with six-pound cannon (cannon were classified by the weight of the ammunition they fired) to deal with heavy defenses; the female was lighter, equipped with only machine

British soldiers test a tank's ability to climb a vertical barrier. Tanks also had to be able to travel four miles per hour on flat ground.

Not Invincible

Although the tank was a powerful new weapon in World War I, it was certainly not invincible. Tanks could be stopped by mud, direct artillery fire, and lucky grenade tosses. In his book *A Company of Tanks*, Major W. H. L. Watson writes about his experiences as the head of the 11th Company of the Tank Corps.

> Bernstein's tank was within reach of the German trenches when a shell hit the cab, decapitated the driver, and exploded in the body of the tank. The corporal was wounded in the arm, and Bernstein was stunned and temporarily blinded. The tank was filled with fumes. As the crew were crawling out, a second shell hit the tank on the roof.
>
> Birkett went forward at top speed, and, escaping the shells, entered the German trenches, where his guns did great execution. The tank was hit twice, and all the crew were wounded, but Birkett went on fighting grimly until his ammunition was exhausted and he himself was badly wounded in the leg. Then at last he turned back. Near the embankment he stopped the tank to take his bearings. As he was climbing out, a shell burst against the side of the tank and wounded him again in the leg. The tank was evacuated. Birkett was brought back on a stretcher, and wounded a third time as he lay on the sunken road outside the [field hospital].
>
> Skinner came right to the edge of an enormous crater and stopped. He tried to reverse, but he could not change gear. The tank was absolutely motionless. The Germans brought up a gun and began to shell the tank. Against field guns he was defenseless if he could not move. With great skill he evacuated his crew, taking his guns with him and the little ammunition that remained.
>
> Swears, the section commander, left the railway embankment, and with the utmost gallantry went forward to look for Skinner. He never came back.
>
> Such were the cheerful reports that I received in my little brick shelter [used as area tank headquarters] by the crossroads.

guns. The male was dubbed "Big Willie," after the chief designer, Major W. G. Wilson; the female was known as "Mother."

Army leaders were more enthusiastic about the new weapons when they saw Big Willie and Mother going through their paces early in 1916. They ordered 150, and because secrecy was so important, it was decided not to refer to them as "landships" or "trench-crossing machines," as some officials had begun calling them. Because of their shape, it was decided that they would be referred to as "tanks"; if anyone asked, they were a new system for storing water near the front.

"The Devil Is Coming"

The tanks made their first battle appearance at the Battle of the Somme on September 15, 1916. The battle had been going on since July 1, with appalling losses of Allied soldiers. And although Swinton had urged General Douglas Haig not to throw away the element of surprise by using the tanks "in driblets"—at less than full strength—Haig was desperate for an edge. Although only 49

Trench Mortars

As the armies huddled down into their trenches, military leaders realized that the long-range artillery pieces they had requested were of little use. What worked was the old trench mortar, a stubby artillery piece—long discarded—that had once been used to lob shells over the walls of fortresses. This excerpt from a soldier's letter (included in Lyn MacDonald's *1914–1918: Voices and Images of the Great War*) shows how feared the mortars were, especially when used with shrapnel shells (those filled with sharp metal scraps).

> In the morning we work in the trenches, in the afternoon generally rest and every other night take turns at sentry-go, either in the bay or an advanced post. The advanced posts are in saps that run out towards the German lines within 20 or 30 yards. One night I was in one of these posts, and it was most exciting. At night you stand with your head above the parapet with a bag of bombs by your side. While I was on, a terrible strafing took place a couple of hundred yards to my right. It was splendid to watch, but as shrapnel fell within a yard or two, it was quite close enough to be unpleasant.
>
> The trench mortars are the things we most dread. They drop right into the trench, and if you are near you don't stand an earthly [chance]. I am getting familiar with the different shells used, but have no wish to become closer acquainted with them. Whizz-bangs are small shells, that don't give you time to say Jack Robinson. All you hear is a whizz and a bang. You automatically duck, but if it is near you it is of no avail. Oil cans are really old oil drums filled with High Explosive and any rubbish they can put in of a killing nature, such as small pieces of iron, steel, and broken bottles. You can see these coming in the daytime, and, depend on it, we give them a wide berth!
>
> Sling bombs, hand and rifle grenades are very similar to our own, and don't do a great deal of damage unless one drops at your feet. The trench mortar shell is like a football on a stick. You can see them coming in the daytime, and at night they are followed by a trail of sparks, so if you keep your eyes open, you have some chance of getting clear.

British troops continue fighting as a trench mortar detonates nearby.

of the ordered 150 tanks had been delivered, Haig decided to send them rumbling toward the German line early that morning.

The results were encouraging, even though seventeen of the forty-nine sent to the front had broken down before reaching the British lines. The thirty-two tanks that did attack were loud and fearsome, and the Germans in their path were terrified. One German war correspondent who witnessed the spectacle wrote,

> When the German troops crept out of their dug-outs in the mist of the morning and stretched their necks to look for the English, their blood chilled. Mysterious monsters were crawling towards them over the craters. . . . Nothing stopped them. . . . Someone in the trenches said, "The devil is coming," and word was passed along the line. Tongues of flame leapt from the side of the iron caterpillars. . . . The English infantry came in waves behind. [35]

Haig and others were pleased with the tanks, despite the mechanical difficulties, and a thousand more were ordered for the Allies. Even so, subsequent models had to address certain problems. For instance, it was necessary to thicken the tank's outer walls. Although bullets weren't able to penetrate the tank's armor, they were causing steel splinters to break loose inside—a definite danger to the crew. Later models needed to be better insulated, too, because the fumes from the engine were so strong that the crew frequently became sick. Better insulation was also necessary because of the noise; the tank's engine was so loud that the crew commander could get the attention of his men only by banging repeatedly on the engine casing with a wrench or hammer.

Although the caterpillar treads made traction good under some circumstances, the muddy crater-scarred terrain of no-man's-land still could stop a tank. Later models were improved by making the treads more deeply patterned and wider. Also, designers added two "crutches." The first of these crutches, called an unditching beam, was strapped onto the top of the tank and could be placed below the treads when faced with deep mud. The second was a fascine, a two-ton bundle of twigs that could be rolled into a deep trench to give the tank extra trench-hopping ability.

Playing an Important Role

A year after the tanks' first appearance at the Somme, no one had seen how effective they could be when used as they were designed to be used. That moment came in late November 1917 at the Battle of Cambrai. Nearly four hundred tanks were assembled, hidden far behind the British line in a wooded area. To drown out the loud clanks of the tanks' engines, Allied planes had been droning for days over the trenches.

To ensure that the offensive would be a surprise, there was no preliminary bombing by artillery. Sending thousands of shells toward enemy trenches was helpful in breaking up some of the barbed wire, but it had been a dead giveaway all throughout the war that an attack was coming. This time, no-man's-land was quiet and undisturbed, and says one witness, "aprons of yet-undefiled barbed wire glinted blue in the sunlight."[36]

At dawn on November 20, the tanks rumbled into action, streaming toward the German trenches in groups of twelve, their machine guns blazing. "Astonished German infantrymen," writes one historian, "accustomed to the days of bombardment that nearly always preceded an attack, fled when they saw giant machines looming out of the mist, each striped with a new camouflage war paint."[37] The Allied infantry followed, and in twelve hours the combination of tanks and foot soldiers pushed the German army back almost seven miles.

Although mistakes were made in the battle, the tanks had done extremely well. One general who had been skeptical about the use of the large vehicles sent a congratulatory telegram to Swinton. "All ranks thank you," he wrote. "Your show."[38] From that day on, tanks were a definite force in finally pushing the Germans into retreat. And even though it was still in its formative stages, military leaders could see that the tank would be an important weapon for future wars.

Chapter 3

The War in the Air

The First World War was not only a war of trenches and mud. All the while that armies first were digging in deep, and then trying to find a way to get the war moving again, conflict was happening in the skies above them. Although World War I was not the first time aircraft were used in battle, it was the testing ground for military aviation. After the war ended, there was no doubt that because of breakthroughs in the use and design of airplanes, combat would never be the same.

Balloons and Airships

Of course, there had been some use of airborne vehicles for years. Hydrogen balloons had been used in the 1860s in the American Civil War; the Union army had an air corps whose job was to organize reconnaissance missions. Tethered at a height of between three hundred and one thousand feet, a balloonist with a telescope could see Confederate troop movement long before soldiers on the ground knew the enemy's whereabouts.

Often the balloonist would make sketches or maps to show what he'd seen. Some balloons were even equipped with light telegraph wires so that an observer could relay messages to soldiers on the ground immediately.

In the years following the Civil War, many European countries became increasingly interested in developing air corps of their own. By the end of the nineteenth century, ballooning units were part of the armies of Russia, Spain, Italy, Germany, Britain, and France. But in the next decade, as the arms buildup increased throughout Europe, any nation eager to use the skies in their war efforts had more choices than simple balloons.

Mixed Reactions to the Wright Brothers

When the Wright brothers kept their little plane aloft for twelve seconds at Kitty Hawk, North Carolina, on December 17, 1903, the event opened up a new category in flying machines. No longer was it necessary to

The Wright brothers make their historic flight on December 17, 1903 (top). Orville Wright and Lieutenant Thomas Selfridge are shown here shortly before their tragic crash (right).

depend on the lifting power of helium or hydrogen. People could now navigate, too, and not have to go simply where the wind blew them.

The idea of a steerable flying machine was intriguing—to some more than others. France and England immediately purchased Wright flyers and set to work modifying and improving them. By 1910, both countries had formed air corps and were training pilots. The United States was less interested in the Wrights' work than Europe was. U.S. military leaders were not impressed with the airplane, believing it to be dangerous and unstable. Their feelings were understandable, for in September 1908, Orville Wright's passenger, Lieutenant Thomas Selfridge, was killed when the plane crashed during a demonstration flight for military leaders.

Fabric and Bailing Wire

When the war began, France and Britain had 187 airplanes of various models, and in

various states of serviceability. Some aircraft had engines in the rear, others in the front. Some were biplanes, with two sets of wings; others were monoplanes, with one set. One thing they all had in common, say historians, was flimsiness.

Most of the planes available in 1914 were little more than frail machines made of plywood held together with lots of bailing wire. The moving parts, such as the rudder or ailerons (the flaps on the plane's wings that control its movement when turning), had to be manually operated. Few planes could achieve a speed of more than fifty miles per hour, and most shook violently when going even that fast.

Safety was almost nonexistent. The pilot sat on a wicker seat located directly over the fuel tank. The "skin" of the plane was fabric coated with a substance called dope, which was highly flammable. There were no brakes, and planes on the ground with engines running had to be held back by a crew until the pilot was ready for takeoff.

A Limited Role

Perhaps because of its physical limitations, the airplane was not considered an important weapon at the outset of the war. It would be used for reconnaissance, just as balloons had been, and perhaps for delivering messages between soldiers at the front and their commanders at headquarters. No aggressive role was seen for Allied airplanes, at least not right away.

But it was soon apparent that airplanes could not do certain things as well as balloons could. For instance, because the balloonist was merely observing, not operating controls and steering as the airplane pilot was, he could better help his artillery below direct their fire accurately. For the same reasons, the balloonist was also in a better position to take long looks at enemy activity on the ground, rather than the short glimpses a pilot was afforded.

The pilot's view was so quick, in fact, that it frequently resulted in incorrect reports. For instance, one pilot had notified his commanders that in one enemy position, the men were "thoroughly disorganized and running around their post in blind panic."[39] The pilot was unaware that he had just flown over a group of soldiers who were taking a break by playing soccer.

On the other hand, the superior mobility of airplanes allowed pilots to accomplish what balloonists could not. Especially when the war stalled in the trenches, it was necessary for observers to cover more ground. Each day planes were sent over enemy lines to try to learn as much as possible about supplies, troops, and artillery. Because they were so much faster than balloons, they were not as easy a target for the infantry.

A Million Pictures

One important tool for many pilots was the aerial camera, which had been used by balloonists for several decades. The large, rectangular cameras were hand-held—easier for a man riding in a balloon to handle

An observer takes a photograph with a hand-held area camera. Technicians later found a way to mount cameras on planes.

than one piloting a plane. However, technicians found a way to mount the camera on the plane, within easy reach of the pilot's left hand. Even more crucial, French scientists greatly improved the camera, enabling it to take serial photographs automatically, one every few seconds, as the plane flew.

This was a vast improvement over anything balloonists could take, for the individual photographs, when put together in the correct sequence, could show a sizeable area of enemy territory that would have been impossible for a tethered balloon to capture on film. Not only was the scope larger, but the new cameras could take pictures from an elevation of ten to fifteen thousand feet, which was obviously much safer for pilots.

By the war's end, Allied pilots had taken more than a million of these photographs. After being assembled by technicians in the correct order, the pictures were distributed to field commanders and leaders at headquarters, who often requested daily updates on new activity on the German line. The lenses could pick up amazing detail from fifteen thousand feet. In fact, the photographs could be magnified to reveal a soldier's footprints in the sand below.

Such detail provided a wealth of information to the Allied command, who were always watchful for a large buildup of heavy artillery, a sure sign of an impending invasion. Even when the Germans had taken pains to camouflage weapons so that they weren't visible to even the most observant pilots, the camera could usually detect them. "A heavy gun painted a dull, neutral color and covered with a few branches," explains one historian, "might avoid detection by a pilot flying his flimsy machine in the face of heavy anti-aircraft fire, but the camera saw the tracks made by the gun moving into position and the heavy shadows cast by the gun itself."[40]

Being a Target

Pilots were taking a risk in gathering this data, for they had to worry about being fired on from the soldiers below. Although it was quite difficult to hit a moving airplane from the ground, an artillery shell passing close to the plane created turbulence that could shake the craft dangerously. Even regular infantry soldiers fired on planes with rifles or machine guns. "You knew the chances were slim they'd hit you if you had any speed at all," recalled one pilot. "But you heard the whizzing of the bullets from machine guns sometimes, and you knew they hadn't missed you by much."[41]

All types of aircraft were plagued by soldiers on the ground taking shots at them. Often this was "friendly fire," a pilot's own army mistakenly shooting at him. Many soldiers shot at anything that flew. The first French air casualty was a hydrogen-filled balloon which was shot full of holes when it flew too low over its own infantry. The balloonist had only done so, he said later, for the purpose of cheering the men up.

Sometimes the reason for mistaken fire was a lack of marking on the plane. As the various countries began painting their flag's

colors or symbols on the aircraft, some of the danger eased. Even so, pilots dreaded any mission that demanded flying low to the ground over either army. One French pilot later recalled being anxious about the arrival of the British Expeditionary Force in France "because up till that moment we had only been fired on by the French. Now we were fired on by French *and* English."[42]

Gradually More Aggressive

Although pilots gathering information were seen by soldiers on the ground as enemies to be attacked, the same animosity did not exist between Allied and German pilots

Flags and symbols were painted on planes to identify them and avoid "friendly fire" from ground troops.

in the air, who enjoyed a sort of peaceful co-existence at the beginning of the war. Most did not carry weapons as they went about their work, and more often than not, they passed each other on reconnaissance missions with a friendly wave. But as the war intensified, the connection pilots felt for one another was shoved aside. Airmen no longer could allow the enemy to continue to cross their lines to gather information without a fight.

An observer mans his gun. The first machine guns mounted on airplanes proved awkward and difficult to use.

Pilots used an assortment of weapons, especially in the early part of the war. Some threw knives or shot off revolvers or rifles at an enemy plane, usually with little success. Many Allied pilots carried long chains with metal hooks that they would dangle down onto a German plane, hoping to catch its propeller or snag one of its wings. One French pilot returned to his airbase with a large hole in his plane and complained that a German pilot had thrown a brick at him.

But the types of weapons on planes improved quickly. Pilots soon progressed from bricks, knives, and chains to the weapon that had made such an impact in the war on the ground, the machine gun.

Machine Guns and Dogfights

The first machine guns on airplanes were mounted behind the observer's seat in twin-cockpit planes. The guns were efficient weapons in the hands of ground soldiers, but in the air they were awkward and difficult to use. They were mounted on brackets made of steel tubing, and in the midst of combat they had a tendency to work themselves loose and fall overboard.

The most difficult aspect of the airplane machine gun was reloading, which was a frequent need since the weapon held only fifty rounds. One or two quick bursts of fire, and the machine gun was empty. That's when the problems really started, according to historian Ezra Bowen:

Reloading in a bucking, swooping aircraft was hard enough for an observer wearing clumsy flight gloves or working with bare, numbed fingers. For a man flying alone it was a gymnastic feat. Holding the stick control with his legs, the pilot had to reach for the drum [holding the ammunition], release it and replace it; all during this time the enemy was either trying to kill him or escape.[43]

Gradually, the difficult-to-load machine guns, such as the French Hotchkiss model and the American-made Lewis, were replaced by the English-made Vickers. The Vickers was in demand on the Allied front; the guns could fire eight hundred rounds per minute and were easier to load. However, the placement of the machine gun had to change so that the frustrated pilot not only had better access to it but could fire it accurately.

Problem Solved . . . Twice

There were two important advances in solving the problem; one was made by an Allied pilot, the other by a German pilot. A Frenchman, Roland Garros, reasoned that the only way he could accurately fire at enemy planes was by shooting them head-on.

The problem with placing a machine gun in front of the pilot is that the pilot would shoot off his propeller.

Garros solved this problem by fitting steel deflector plates at an angle on the blades of the propeller; any bullets that struck the blades would harmlessly bounce off. Greatly enthused by his breakthrough, Garros went on what one historian calls "a very short-lived rampage, sowing death, destruction, and above all, terror among the German airmen in his area."[44]

Understandably, the German army was furiously trying to understand how the French pilot was shooting down their planes, one after another. Eventually his secret was found out when, after engine trouble he was forced to land behind German lines. Before he could set his plane on fire (the standard operating procedure when using a weapon the Germans did not have), he was captured. The plane was put into the hands of a Dutch designer named Anthony Fokker, who improved on Garros's idea.

Interestingly, Fokker saw that Garros had merely been lucky. Any one of the bullets he'd been firing could have deflected backward off the propeller and killed him. Fokker invented a means of controlling the fire of a machine gun with an interrupter gear. This kept the gun from firing when one of the propeller's blades was in the way. Putting the propeller–machine-gun assembly onto one of his own planes (a new design that could go an amazing eighty miles per hour), Fokker had come up with the first reliable fighter plane.

Though the Allies had once enjoyed superiority in the air, the German pilots lucky enough to have a new Fokker plane could now without a doubt claim it. Complaining that they were "Fokker fodder," Allied pilots watched as their numbers decreased—shot out of the sky by the new planes with high-powered machine guns. Eventually, however, a Fokker was forced to land behind Allied lines, and after taking it apart and studying it, the Allied technicians produced comparable planes.

Monsters of the Sky

Fokker's work enabled Germany to advance quickly in the air war. However, Germany

A German Fokker closes in for the kill on a British fighter.

had not begun the war with much interest in airplanes. Although the Germans had purchased several, the German military was far more intrigued with a different sort of aircraft. A retired army colonel, Count Ferdinand von Zeppelin, had been working on the design of huge, cigar-shaped airships. Subsequently known as zeppelins, these airships were similar to large balloons, since they could be filled with hydrogen gas.

However, the zeppelin was an improvement over the balloon because it was powered by engine-driven propellers that were suspended—along with a crew of up to twenty—in a gondola from the balloon itself. The five-hundred-foot-long craft had fabric walls supported by an aluminum frame. Because of the enormous amount of hydrogen gas inflating the zeppelin, it could fly much higher than airplanes or the earlier balloons.

By the beginning of the war, Germany had built twenty-six zeppelins. Count Zeppelin was confident that his airships would help Germany win the war. Rather than use them for reconnaissance, however, he planned a more aggressive role. Equipped with machine guns and the capacity for more than a ton of bombs, the zeppelin would become one of the most feared sights of the war, resulting in a flurry of antiaircraft weaponry by the Allies.

"Zeppelin, Flieg!"

Early in the war, zeppelins began making night flights across the English Channel to Britain, where they dropped their loads of

"You Feel Naked and Helpless"

The German Fokker plane (introduced in April 1918) was so much better than any other plane that Allied pilots usually felt as though they had no chance at all in a one-on-one fight. Most respected was the Fokker D-VII, a bright blue and red biplane with black crosses on its wings and tail. It was so powerful and technically superior that it was the only plane that the armistice agreement after the war specifically mentioned to be surrendered by the German army. The following excerpt is from Ezra Bowen's book *Knights of the Air*.

> In January 1916, Royal Flying Corps headquarters issued this rather desperate order: "Until the Royal Flying Corps are in possession of a machine as good or better than the German Fokker . . . it must be laid down as a hard and fast rule that a machine proceeding on reconnaissance must be escorted by at least three fighting machines."

One British airman sent home a vivid description of what it was like when a Fokker approached. "You feel naked and helpless. The panic seeps through your pores . . . everything seems unreal . . . and then you hear the guns hacking. All I can do at the controls is stay to a westerly course and summon every trick I know . . . swerving erratically from side to side so the [plane] does not have a steady target. Only as a last shift do I give away altitude, since he can climb like an arrow off a bowstring and enjoys an absolute advantage if I go too low. . . . It is a harrowing, execrable ordeal."

bombs on various targets. Although the death toll caused by such bombing raids was about six hundred people—far less than that caused by other weapons—it was the first time that civilians behind the war's front had been attacked. One bomb dropped on the East End of London landed on a kindergarten, killing twenty children. Others hit factories, apartment buildings, and assorted civilian targets.

The zeppelin's raids of the First World War marked a critical moment in warfare, say historians. Write Jay Winter and Blaine Baggett, "In 1914–18 a boundary was crossed—the boundary between war on fixed sights and units—cities, armed camps, strongpoints, depots—and war on entire populations."[45] Colorful picture postcards that circulated in Germany show artists' renditions of Londoners panicking as a zeppelin hovers high above. A popular children's song of 1914 celebrated Germany's newest weapon, and what it would accomplish:

"Zeppelin, flieg,
Hilf uns im Krieg
Flieg nach England
England wird abgebrannt,
Zeppelin, flieg!"

"Zeppelin, fly,
Help us in the war,
Fly to England,
England shall be destroyed with fire,
Zeppelin, fly!"[46]

This so-called strategic bombing resulted in a loss of morale among the people of Britain. The knowledge that one of the monstrous airships could appear without warning in the night sky—the ships flew at such high altitudes that their engines could rarely be heard—was terrifying. Fear of attack by zeppelins was widespread not only in Britain and France but even in the United States, which was far out of the craft's range.

The Need for Appropriate Weapons

Even more terrifying than the attacks themselves was the feeling that Britain could not defend itself from the zeppelins' bombs. The Allies had enough airplanes to chase the airships, but flying at night was dangerous and was almost never done. Besides the difficulty caused by darkness, the airplanes faced another disadvantage: They could not catch the zeppelins because they could not fly as high. Airplanes in 1915 struggled to attain an altitude of fifteen thousand feet, while a huge airship could easily soar to over sixteen thousand feet, even with its full payload of bombs. Once it had dropped all of its bombs, a zeppelin could rise to almost five miles as its crews breathed from bottles of pure compressed oxygen.

As bleak as the Allies' predicament seemed, however, weapons experts quickly rose to the occasion. The Royal Navy

The zeppelin, carrying more than a ton of bombs, became one of the most feared sights of the war.

Tactics in the Air

One of the best-known Allied pilots of World War I was a Canadian named William (Billy) Bishop, who was described by a fellow ace as being "incapable of fear." In his book *Winged Warfare*, Bishop describes the most important things a fighter pilot of the Great War had to remember.

> When flying alone or with just one other, it is always a case of constantly turning around in your seat, turning your machine to right or left, looking above and around or below you all the time. It is a very tiring piece of work, so it is but natural that when you have three or four other men behind you, you spend more time looking in the direction where you hope the enemy machines are, if you want to attack them, and to looking at any interesting sights which are on the ground.

> In ordinary fight or duel we had tactics, of course, to suit the occasion. The great thing is never to let the enemy's machine get behind you, or "on your tail." Once he reaches there it is very hard to get him off, as every turn and every move you make, he makes with you.

> By the same token, it is exactly the position into which you wish to get, and once there you must constantly strive for a shot as well as look out for attacks from other machines that may be near. It is well if you are against odds never to stay long after one machine. If you concentrate on him for more than a fraction of a second, some other [German] has a chance to get a steady shot at you, without taking any risks himself.

> To hit a machine when it is flying at right angles to you across your nose is very hard. It requires a good deal of judgment in knowing just how far ahead of him to aim. It is necessary to hit the pilot himself and not the machine to be successful, and also necessary to hit the pilot in the upper part of the body where it will be more certain to put him completely out of action at once. When a machine goes into flames it is largely a matter of luck, as it means that several of your bullets have pierced the petrol tank and ignited the vapor escaping from it.

brought several thirteen-pound guns (the number refers to the weight of the shell the guns fired) to be used in London. These were loaded onto truck beds and moved throughout the city when needed. Strong searchlights were also mobilized; these could throw beams of bright light on a zeppelin, giving antiaircraft gunners a more accurate target.

Allied aircraft were also improved. Faster planes, such as the British-made Martinsyde-Scout, were pushed through production. Although a zeppelin could still get away by increasing its altitude, there were times when bad weather or a hit from an artillery shell kept it low enough for the pilots to catch it. In those instances, the Allied pilots had an assortment of new weapons at their fingertips.

The most vulnerable aspect of the zeppelin was the flammable gas that filled it; therefore, the new Allied weapons were fire-producing, or incendiary. For the first time, pilots were given loads of incendiary bombs of various sorts to use when chasing zeppelins. In addition, their machine guns were loaded with a new explosive bullet containing phosphorus, a weapon that was so efficient in blowing fiery holes in the zeppelins that it was categorized by one German airman as "an invention of the devil."[47]

The Human Weapons

From this more aggressive use of airplanes emerged a whole new type of "weapon"—the pilots themselves. Although they were fighting the same war as other soldiers, they fought in an arena that everyone could see, in machines that were so new that most people on the planet had never set eyes on one in the air. "Up there, a man's daring, or lack of it, was visible to all," writes one historian, "and the issues were quickly resolved. The battle ended when the loser crashed to earth while the victor was still flying high."[48]

The pilots were young; the average age of an Allied pilot was twenty. Almost no one who signed on in the French or British air service at the beginning of the war had ever flown an airplane, or even ridden in one. They received training in hastily organized flight schools. Most flew their first missions with fewer than fifteen hours in the air, and some had as little as five.

In that small amount of time, however, they had to learn looping, spinning, and various climbing turns in addition to shooting from a moving plane. With so much expected of them and so little time to accomplish it, it is not hard to understand why 60 percent of Allied air deaths during the war occurred during training.

After a pilot was through with his train-ing, his life expectancy at the front was three to five weeks. Often, pilots wrote in their journals of young men who took off for their first mission and died within ten or fifteen minutes.

Yet despite such grim odds, as well as such a short time to learn how to fly, the idea of being a pilot was glorious to many young men. It was colorful, wild, and reckless; the inherent danger made flying seem more like a true test of bravery. Prime Minister Lloyd George of Britain compared the flyers to the knights of old: "They recall the legendary days of chivalry, not merely by the daring of their exploits but by the nobility of their spirit."[49]

A Varied and Independent Lot

There were degrees of proficiency in being a pilot. An "ace" was a pilot who had downed at least five enemy planes; Germans called him a *kanone*, or "big gun." However he was known, it was every pilot's aspiration to be part of that elite set. (Although many British pilots were "aces," the term was unofficial for them because the British military did not like singling its men out in that way.)

Part of the pilots' allure was their colorful, sometimes eccentric manner. Unlike other soldiers who were required to dress in regulation uniforms, the pilots wore what they liked. Some wore a long bright scarf or a school sweater. One French pilot wore a black leather jacket over his blue pajamas—he said the outfit relaxed him. A British pilot flew missions with his pet monkey sitting in the seat next to him.

Their eccentricities did not keep them from their attention to duty, however. With calm and self-control, the aces were masters of evasive turns and spins, attacking, and aim—the latter being extremely difficult in a small airplane. The pilots kept careful record of their statistics, and those with higher totals than other pilots were considered heroes among civilians, who loved hearing about their exploits. One famous ace remembered being stunned when he met a little boy who could recite his statistics, with details about each of the planes he'd shot down. "In a ghastly war of death and maiming, lice and dysentery, poison gas and jagged iron," comments one historian, "the knights of the air appeared to offer some redeeming quality."[50]

Bringing on the Bombers

With these weapons, the Allies were finally able to minimize the threat of zeppelin raids. Some of the mighty airships were shot down; others were destroyed by air-to-ground bombing missions. And even though the German military decided to discontinue zeppelin raids by the end of 1916, bombing did not stop. Bombing London had diverted guns and planes away from the fighting on the western

---

America Unprepared

Although American pilots contributed a great deal to the war effort (many flew in French squadrons before the United States entered the war), America contributed very little to the making and designing of airplanes. In this excerpt from James L. Stokesbury's *A Short History of Air Power*, the author examines the state of the American aviation industry in 1917.

American military aviation was in as immature a state as the army generally. Most of what had been happening in Europe during the war years had passed the United States by. The vast excitement over the war had not been translated into action, and the American government had remained determinedly uninterested in warlike postures. . . . In 1914 Congress had established an Aviation Section of the Signal Corps of the U.S. Army, but with an authorized strength of 60 officers and 260 enlisted men, this was not a very important element in the overall picture. In the summer of 1916 the army had engaged in a rough lit-

tle campaign on the Mexican border, against the famous bandit Pancho Villa. The aerial contingent in this operation, one squadron, was useless. It lost all its planes to winds, dust storms, and Mexican conditions, and it achieved nothing. . . .

Congress voted 13 million dollars for expansion [in 1916] and eight months later, when the country went to war, the Aviation section had 131 officers, 1,087 enlisted men, and about 250 airplanes, not one of which was combat worthy by European standards. At this point the British and the French, who up till now had refused to release any useful information to the Americans, sent over high-powered aviation missions to get things moving. The French came up with, and the Americans accepted, a plan to build 22,000 aircraft, plus 80 percent spare parts and 44,000 aircraft engines. . . [but] the infant American aircraft industry, though it expanded rapidly, never came near these stratospheric figures.

---

front, so it was to Germany's advantage to continue it. In response, Allied pilots began the aerial bombing of German cities, as well as field targets such as supply trains, ammunitions storehouses, and even ships.

For such bombing missions, pilots used planes that were different from the ones used in reconnaissance. Both Allied and German technicians had worked hard, hurrying along new designs for planes with sturdier frames and for engines powerful enough to more than double the speed of the planes first used in 1914. In addition to being faster, many of these planes could carry more than a ton of bombs, and their increased gas tank capacity allowed them to fly farther into enemy territory.

One of the largest bombers was the Caproni, made in Italy. Weighing seven tons, the Caproni could fly for seven hours and had a wingspan of ninety-eight feet—a monster compared with the little planes

used by pilots for reconnaissance and fighting. A British bomber called the Handley-Page was another improvement. Nicknamed the "Bloody Paralyzer" because of its size and bomb capacity, the Handley-Page could fly at an amazing one hundred miles per hour.

New Tools for Defense

The increase in bombing raids resulted in some improvements in the defense against bombers, too. In London, where most of the strategic bombing was occurring, the Allies added antiaircraft guns. The thirteen-pound guns, which had been quickly deployed to London during the first zeppelin raids, were replaced by eighteen-pounders. These were more effective, sending shells

The Caproni, with a ninety-eight foot wingspan that made it one of the largest bombers of the war, could fly for seven hours.

more than two thousand yards farther than the thirteen-pounders. Once again, since these guns were in short supply, they were mounted on truck beds and driven to various parts of London during raids.

Great strides were also made in warning citizens. At first there had been no organized plan of how to alert people, and the methods the city seized on seem almost laughable. "Early attempts to warn the civilian population of an impending aerial attack," says one expert, "included firing rockets and bicycle-mounted policemen wearing placards reading 'Police Notice— Take Cover.'"[51] By late 1917 a London manufacturer created piercingly loud air horns, which could warn citizens to take cover.

One of the most interesting plans to protect the metropolitan area of London from bombs was the installation of steel curtains that were suspended from stationary kite balloons. Several of the balloons would be tethered with a web of steel cables suspended from them. Any bomber making a low pass to drop its payload would not see the curtain until it was too late, and would be destroyed before it could do any damage. There is no record of any German bomber over Britain being destroyed by the curtain; however, the same plan was implemented by the British over the Suez Canal during the war, with notable success.

A Strong Weapon of Future Wars

The airplane, though not a dominant, decisive weapon in World War I, nevertheless showed its potential very clearly. Airplanes evolved rapidly during the war—not only because of the technicians who designed them but because of the creativity and bravery of the pilots who flew them. Beginning as merely vehicles for spotters and observers, airplanes became machines of war. Bombing, critical aerial reconnaissance behind enemy lines, and tactical support of infantry and artillery—all of these were demonstrated as the future of war, even if they had not been mastered by 1918.

Chapter 4

The War on the Sea

While air warfare was a new field in World War I, naval power was a mainstay—especially for Britain, which was the undisputed leader on the seas. For three centuries, no nation could match Britain when it came to the design and building of ships. The skill and discipline of the crews of the Royal Navy were unsurpassed, too. Even with its long-standing superiority at sea, however, Britain joined other European nations that were beefing up their naval power in the years before World War I.

Britain had modernized a great deal of its navy in the early years of the twentieth century, using a new material for building the Royal Fleet. The ships used in the American Civil War, the *Monitor* and the *Merrimack*, had shown the advantages of metal armor over traditional wood, and modern shipbuilding had taken a lesson. Artillery shells had sunk or set fire to wooden ships, but they could do little damage to one with several inches of iron protection.

Though the British had the clear edge in naval matters, Kaiser Wilhelm of Germany decided to challenge them by ordering larger, more modern ships for his navy. Germany's industrial centers certainly had the capacity to build them, for Germany was producing twice the amount of steel that Britain was. Kaiser Wilhelm was confident that a German advantage at sea could mean an early victory when war finally did break out.

The Birth of the Dreadnoughts

Britain's response to Germany's challenge was a powerful new weapon—a warship that, when it was launched in February 1906, made all other warships obsolete. It was named *Dreadnought*, a name that would henceforth refer to an entire class of warships. The *Dreadnought* had ten large-caliber guns, the most of any ship ever made and it had thick armored plating. Although it was heavier than other ships, it could reach a speed of twenty-one knots—three knots faster than any existing battleship. Unlike earlier warships, it was powered by oil, which was much cleaner and more efficient than coal; ships using oil would have to refuel less often. The *Dreadnought* was followed by ten more ships of the new dreadnought class, each bigger and more powerful than the last. The final dreadnought ship, built in 1911, had fourteen large guns, and its armor was eleven inches thick.

The dreadnoughts were a source of great pride to the British people, who saw them as the newest proof of their nation's naval excellence. Military analyst Robert O'Connell says that part of the charm of these giant ships was the paradox of power and beauty they presented:

> Great floating fortresses, guns bristling from slab-sided turrets, crowned with massive steel superstructures, they literally oozed defiance. When viewed from either end they were squat and immovable as castles. Yet they almost appeared delicate and graceful when seen lengthwise.[52]

Dreadnaught-class battleships, such as the British HMS Centurion, *made all other warships obsolete.*

Soon other nations followed with dreadnought ships of their own, including Germany, who built seventeen of the ships between 1909 and 1914, and the United States. Before the war began, Britain even turned out a number of "superdreadnoughts" that had even more heavy artillery, including a large number of antiaircraft guns.

"A Weapon *Must* Be Expendable"
At the beginning of the war, most military leaders assumed that a great deal of important fighting would take place on the sea. It was believed that confrontation between Britain and Germany would come early.

In the North Sea, where the majority of the ships were located, first the British and then the Germans would use one of their smaller ships as "bait," hoping to draw in the enemy's fleet and then attack them. But by the spring of 1916, there had been no large battles between the two navies. The dreadnoughts, their crews spoiling for a fight, were idle, as both navies seemed to be more interested in keeping out of one another's way than in fighting.

The problem was the dreadnoughts—the very weapon that experts had predicted as a major factor in the war. Neither the British nor the Germans were willing to risk losing one of their giant warships, and for that reason neither side used them aggressively. One military historian says that because the huge, expensive ships were usually named after a national hero or a great military victory, they became far too symbolic.

"For this reason alone," he maintains, "the loss of one came to be thought of as a minor national disaster that could seriously affect the morale of the armed forces, as well as of the general public."[53]

Thus, the dreadnoughts spent the first two years of the war shielded by smaller, lighter ships in their fleets. And while the dreadnoughts might have been decisive early on had one naval commander or another decided to use them, no one did. Stresses one expert, "to be of use in war . . . a weapon *must* be expendable."[54]

"Something Wrong with Our Bloody Ships"
The one large naval engagement of the war occurred on May 31, 1916, in the North Sea off the coast of Jutland in Denmark. It was an important battle, even though there was no clear-cut winner or loser. The result of the Battle of Jutland was that both sides changed their minds about the weapons most important for a navy.

A small force of forty German ships met a fifty-two–ship section of the British fleet, and both sides' warships began firing on one another. Though the Germans were clearly the underdog, they did a great amount of damage, quickly turning two of Britain's dreadnoughts into fireballs with their big guns. Admiral David Beatty, commanding that segment of the British fleet, complained to another officer, "There seems to be something wrong with our bloody ships today."[55]

There *was* something wrong, and the British should have known it. A poorly de-

HMS Inflexible *picks up survivors of a sunken dreadnaught during the Battle of Jutland (top). British battleships line up to fire on the German fleet during the same engagement (right).*

signed turret on the dreadnoughts left the magazine (the large supply of shells below the guns) exposed. Any explosion hitting the turret would travel down to the shells and ignite them. The Germans had noted the design flaw and had corrected it, adding a double door of metal over the magazine to protect it. The British navy, however, had not noticed the error, and as a result, lost two warships—with twenty-four hundred men.

New Thinking About Weapons at Sea

The fight drew more sections of the British and German fleets; in all, 252 ships clashed in the twelve-hour battle. Damage was done

to both sides as heavy artillery sent shells thundering back and forth. The Germans finally left, realizing that their smaller fleet could not continue to sustain the losses they were suffering.

But even though the German navy retreated, the final statistics show that the British suffered the most losses—sixty-one hundred men and fourteen ships. Three of these were dreadnoughts. The Germans had lost twenty-five hundred men and eleven ships, only one of which was a large warship.

The British naval commander was widely criticized for failing to follow the German fleet and finishing it off. However, he insisted that he did not want to risk losing any more of his own fleet, especially the large warships. For all he knew, the German navy could have been leading him into a minefield or a torpedo attack. Had that happened, he maintained, the British certainly would have lost control of the seas.

Besides being the last time the two fleets would meet in the First World War, Jutland marked the end of a naval era when ships were judged on their size and strength. Just as new weapons such as the machine gun had forced both armies to alter the way they fought, the navies, too, had to change. The weapons that now mattered most did their work under the surface of the sea.

"Underhand, Unfair . . . Un-English"

Before World War I, the submarine had appeared in two American wars. In the Revolutionary War, a farmer named David Bushnell had taken his little submergible craft called the *Turtle* into New York Harbor, hoping to sneak up on an English ship and sink it. During the Civil War, Confederates used a slightly more sophisticated underwater boat, the *Hunley*. Unlike the *Turtle*, the *Hunley* was able to sink its prey; unfortunately, the heavy Union ship sank on top of the little submarine, carrying its crew to their deaths.

The submarines of the pre–World War I era were much improved. They were larger than their predecessors, weighing around five hundred tons, and could cruise on the water's surface at almost the same speed as most merchant ships. They had two large ballast tanks across the hull that controlled the intake and outflow of air or water, thus regulating the submarine's floating or diving. Most submarines could stay underwater for twenty-four hours at a time, and carried several tubes for firing torpedoes, or underwater explosive missiles.

Britain possessed the most submarines at the beginning of the war, with seventy-four; even so, its leaders were scornful of underwater craft. In much the same way they viewed mines and poison gas, British officials deemed the submarine "underhand, unfair, and damned un-English."[56] British military leaders decided that the best use for submarines—if they were to be used at all—was as a means of defense. If the coast of Britain or France should come under attack, they acknowledged, a fleet of submarines could be useful in repelling it.

U-Boats

Germany was far behind the British in developing the submarine. Because German naval leaders considered the submarine a defensive weapon, they were uninterested in it, preferring to spend their money on ships that could be used to attack. As one high-ranking admiral declared, "I refuse to throw money away on submarines so long as they could only cruise in home waters."[57]

As a result, Germany had only twenty submarines, which were known as U-boats (from *Unterseebooten*, or "undersea boats"), when the First World War began. Those twenty, however, were superior to those of the British. By adding a more streamlined second hull over the ballast tanks of the original hull, engineers had created a craft that could cut through waves like a regular ship. This meant that the U-boats were far more stable on the surface, where submarines spent the majority of their time at sea. The British subs with their single hulls were bumpy and choppy—a source of great discomfort to the crew. Besides changing the design of their submarines, the German navy found new uses for them. They gave U-boat crews permission to prowl the waters of the North Sea in war patrols against British ships.

It did not take long for both sides to see how powerful a weapon the submarine could be. On September 22, 1914, just twenty miles off the Dutch coast, one single German U-boat fired its torpedoes on three large British cruisers, sinking them. The cruisers weighed a total of 36,000 tons and had 1,460 men on board; in terms of casualties, it was the greatest disaster the British navy had suffered in almost three hundred years. No longer would submarines be considered weapons of defense.

German U-boats prepare to go to sea. Stable and streamlined, they proved a valuable offensive weapon against the British navy.

For the British, the most frightening aspect of the event was the obvious change in the way navies fought. "Nothing that had yet occurred had so emphatically proclaimed the change that had come over naval warfare," writes one British historian, "and never perhaps had so great a result been obtained by means so relatively small."[58]

To Unrestricted Warfare

German U-boats became an even more powerful weapon early in 1915, when they began targeting nonmilitary boats as well as military ones. Angered over the blockade the British navy had imposed on Germany to prevent weapons and other matériel from reaching its ports, the German commanders authorized the sinking of merchant ships bound for Britain, even those from neutral countries. Said Kaiser Wilhelm, "We will frighten the British flag off the face of the waters and starve the British people until they, who have refused peace, will kneel and plead for it."[59]

This move to unrestricted warfare had both positive and negative results for Germany. On the positive side, Germans were able to greatly curtail the merchandise finding its way to British ports. Any ship that wanted to trade or do business with Britain was at risk in the war zone of the North Sea. In August 1915, the U-boats sank 185,000 tons of shipping, and the totals continued to skyrocket. In April 1917, German U-boats sank an amazing 950,000 tons of shipping. Approximately one out of every four merchant ships leaving Britain was sunk.

Not surprisingly, Great Britain experienced severe shortages of food, oil, and other important commodities because of the unrestricted submarine warfare.

The *Lusitania*

On the other hand, Germany's U-boat campaign was one of the factors that brought the United States into the war. On May 7, 1915, the British passenger liner *Lusitania* was on its way from New York City to Britain when it was torpedoed by a U-boat. Nearly twelve hundred people, ninety-four of them children, were killed.

The sinking of the *Lusitania* brought a storm of outrage throughout much of the world, especially in the United States, since 138 of the victims had been Americans. President Woodrow Wilson cried when he was told the news. A fuming Theodore Roosevelt denounced the German navy's action as "piracy on a vaster scale of murder than any old-time pirate ever practiced."[60]

The United States issued a stern ultimatum: Germany was to stop its unrestricted warfare campaign or else the United States would break off diplomatic relations with Germany, a very serious step. Not willing to see the United States enter the war, Germany complied, halting its attacks on merchant and passenger vessels for the time being (unrestricted submarine warfare would resume during the last several months of the war in 1917). Interestingly, many historians feel that had Germany ignored public outrage and continued with its blockade

The sinking of the passenger ship Lusitania *was a major reason why the United States entered the war.*

and unrestricted U-boat warfare, it could very well have won the war by the beginning of 1916.

Seagulls, Seals, and "Ears"

The U-boats' success—whether stalking merchant vessels or Allied navy ships—energized the German navy. German shipbuilders began producing more; by the war's end, 141 more U-boats would be launched. With so many U-boats hiding beneath the surface of the sea, Allied naval officials were at a loss. How, they wondered, could they fight an enemy they could not see?

Weapons experts got to work devising plans, and some of their ideas were laugh-

able. For instance, some animal handlers believed that seagulls could be trained to seek U-boat periscopes and perch atop them, thereby alerting nearby Allied ships. A similar suggestion was that pods of seals could be trained to locate submarines. Six seals from a London stage show gave it a try, but the results were disappointing. The seals, says naval strategist Bernard Brodie, "shrewdly appraised U-boats as inedible, or

Inside the Submarine

Living so close together for months at a time was difficult for all soldiers, but it was probably most profound for submarine crews. With no opportunity to get away from other people, even for a minute or two, the sailors on submarines had to get used to a wide variety of dangers, hardships, and annoyances, as Douglas Botting explains in this excerpt from *The U-Boats*.

In a true Atlantic storm the water would break over the bridge as solid as wet cement. The force and weight of the seas was so great that on occasion men were swept overboard. In such weather, the view from the bridge was petrifying—a vast wilderness of mountainous waves whipped white by the roaring wind. The duration of bridge watches had to be cut by half in these storms, for no man could stand more than two hours of battering by the seas and laceration by spray. Conditions were little better belowdecks. The violent corkscrewing, rolling, pitching and yawing motions of the boat, the brutal jolt as the bow hit a wave, and the steam-hammer clang of the sea smashing down on the hull made it difficult to relax for a minute.

Whether the U-boat was on the surface or was submerged, the interior lights burned 24 hours round the clock, effectively blurring the distinction between day and night. On long patrols especially, crews lived in an atmosphere of increasing squalor. The heat was oppressive, the air stale and foul and reeking of bilge water, wet oilskins, rubber boots, sweat and diesel fumes so thick that a man's hair became a pitchy mire.

The U-boat grew steadily damper from the intense condensation and the frequent leakage of water through the hatch of the conning tower. Bunks smelled moldy and charts began to rot. A gray-green film of mildew coated shoes and shirts. Sausages sprouted luxurious overcoats of mold overnight. In this environment a man could easily grow irritable and morose and, under stress, even paranoiac or violent—*Blechkoller* it was called, tin-can neurosis.

The difficult day-to-day living conditions on submarines were compounded during surface patrols in stormy weather.

at any rate unsavory, and declined to waste effort upon them."[61]

Not all of the ideas were worthless, however. One that showed great promise was not so much a weapon as it was a locating device. The hydrophone—or as it was known to sailors of the First World War, "ears"—was an American invention that picked up the sounds of a submarine underwater and transmitted them to a ship nearby. Water is an excellent conductor of sound, and with practice, an operator could tell the difference between the sounds of the propellers of various types of ships.

Allied subchasers (small, lightweight craft that were armed with hydrophones) usually worked in teams of three. With information from each of the subchasers, engineers could determine the direction and speed of a U-boat. Once that information was known, Allied ships could attempt to destroy the U-boat, using the newest antisubmarine weapon in their arsenal—the depth charge.

The Depth Charge

Nicknamed "ash cans," depth charges were actually cannisters of TNT fitted with a special mechanism that would set off the explosive at a preset depth. Even though a U-boat was a deadly weapon, it was actually more vulnerable than one might think. The steel that surrounded it was very thin and cracked easily.

The depth charge did not have to hit a U-boat directly to destroy it. One historian describes the physical effects of a destroyer's

Depth charges could destroy a U-boat from as far away as one hundred feet.

depth charge that came within one hundred feet of a submarine:

> An explosion . . . sent a stone-hard wall of water crashing against the hull. . . . Moments later a shock wave struck their boat with the *clang* of a sledge hammer on an anvil. The U-boat then shook crazily, vibrating from stem to stern. Fuel lines snapped. Light bulbs shattered,

The Convoy, a Weapon of Defense

Although Q-ships, dazzle paint, and other anti-submarine measures helped thwart U-boat attacks, in 1917 the subs were still preying on Allied and neutral ships. Many of the ships were laden with food, fuel, and matériel needed by British civilians and soldiers alike. So heavy were the losses, in fact, that British leaders were privately estimating that they could not go on more than six or seven weeks. If they did not get supplies soon, they would be forced to surrender to Germany.

Several military leaders raised the idea of convoys. An old method, it simply meant that supply ships would be accompanied by larger, more heavily armed ships, based on the notion of "safety in numbers." U-boats would be wary of attacking a ship if they knew they would almost certainly be sunk, too.

Interestingly, many British navy men scoffed at the idea. It seemed too defensive for them, hardly the image the Royal Navy wished to project. Why, they asked, should they waste their best battleships

doing defensive work? As historian Richard Hough explains in *The Great War at Sea*, the argument seemed foolish to traditional navy men: "To protect merchantmen, to scurry about them like a sheepdog, was *defensive*. To send out hundreds of men o'war to hunt down and destroy commerce raiders was *offensive*."

But since few of the British battleships were hunting down U-boats, and since no other idea seemed to work well enough, the convoy system was finally tried. An experimental convoy in May 1917 traveled from the Mediterranean Sea to Britain. Eight or nine destroyers and cruisers accompanied several heavily laden merchant ships. Not one ship was sunk.

The convoy system proved to be the antisubmarine tactic that ended the U-boats' dominance. The number of ships sunk fell dramatically; out of eight hundred ships convoyed in July and August 1917, only five were lost. The entry of the United States into the war also helped, since its destroyers became available for convoy duty too.

plunging the vessel into darkness. Instruments went wild. The hull sprang leaks, or burst open suddenly, drowning everyone.[62]

Occasionally, the captain of a U-boat that had narrowly escaped being destroyed by a depth charge found that his only escape was pretending to be hit. He might use his torpedo tubes to blow clothing or other items to the surface, or release oil, hoping to fool the destroyer's crew into believing he'd been blown up. Historians maintain, however, that even when such an act was successful and a destroyer did leave the scene without firing more depth charges, the psychological dam-

age to the U-boat's crew was enormous. For weeks and months afterward, many men would suffer from nightmares, hallucinations, and other symptoms, making them completely unfit for further duty in such precarious situations.

Q-Ships and Dazzle Camouflage

One of the most interesting weapons the Allies devised in their war with U-boats was the Q-ship. During the time that Germany was waging unrestricted submarine warfare, U-boats attacked civilian and military ships differently. When attacking a merchant vessel, a U-boat would not stay below the surface and fire torpedoes, as it did when attacking a warship. Instead, it would surface and shoot its deck guns, saving its torpedoes for a more dangerous target, such as a battleship.

To take advantage of the U-boat's vulnerability at such times, Britain disguised some warships as merchant vessels, hiding the large guns under deckhouses or lifeboats. When the U-boat surfaced, the sailors (dressed as merchant seamen) would quickly open fire. Several U-boats were sunk in this manner, and it is impossible to know how many others were spared because a German captain did not want to risk a confrontation with a ship he wasn't sure of.

Camouflage was used in other ways, too. As the Allies began to panic at the large number of ships being lost to U-boat warfare, France and Britain called on their artists, designers, and architects for help in making their ships as confusing as possible to an observer. The answer was called "dazzle camouflage," a method of painting that fools the eye.

Bold geometric shapes in a variety of colors painted on the sides of a warship made it difficult for a distant observer to tell what kind of ship it was, how fast it was moving, and even in what direction it was going. A ship might have a false wake painted on its side to give the impression that it was traveling very fast—thereby making it more difficult for the U-boat to accurately fire a torpedo—or have bold crisscrossing bars masking the vessel's silhouette. Other ships were painted a neutral sea color, with a small boat painted on the side going the opposite direction.

The American Contribution

Though each of these tricks no doubt saved some ships, when Germany resumed its unrestricted submarine warfare in 1917, the Allies were in serious trouble. They were building warships as fast as they could, but they could not keep pace with the numbers that were being sunk each week by the U-boats.

The entry of the United States into the war added a great deal to the antisubmarine campaign being waged by the Allies. For one thing, the United States had a large number of destroyers—light, fast ships that

American destroyers pass through the Panama Canal on their way to fight German U-boats in the Atlantic.

could outmaneuver a U-boat on the surface. Destroyers were less likely than other ships to be torpedoed since they rode very high in the water. But they were not immune, and the long months of U-boat attacks had depleted many of the British destroyers. By early 1918, about eighty American destroyers were on duty in the North Sea.

Another contribution of the U.S. navy was a new type of mine, or underwater explosive. For years the British had laid minefields around presumed U-boat areas, but with little success. A large number of British mines had faulty firing apparatuses and did not explode when they should. Even those that might work were rarely put to the test, for a skilled U-boat captain was able to maneuver underneath the large mines and thereby avoid catastrophe.

But an American-made mine with sensitive antennae stretching out thirty-five feet in all directions made avoiding mines almost impossible. American and British ships mined a 250-mile area between Scotland and Norway—Germany's entrance to the North Sea. More than seventy thousand of the new mines were laid in what was at the time the greatest mine-laying mission ever accomplished. The U-boats were effectively trapped in their own bases, although, writes one weapons expert, "[the minefield's] value as a psychological deterrent to jittery U-boat commanders was probably greater than its success in trapping submarines."[63]

The war at sea, originally thought to be a part of the war that clearly favored the Allies, had been controlled not by the mighty dreadnoughts but by the U-boat. It would be the naval weapon that would endure, playing an equally important role in the next war.

Chapter 5

The Secret War

Espionage, or the secretive accumulation of information about the enemy, can often make a big difference in a war. Having advance notice that the other side is planning an attack, for example, allows a commander to request additional troops and weapons. Knowing the exact location of the enemy's lethal underwater mines can help the captain of a warship avoid disaster.

There have been spies in wars since ancient times, and the First World War was no exception. In fact, espionage played a key role in the outcome of the war—and was largely responsible for the United States entering the war at all. But as crucial a weapon as the gathering and passing on of information was in the First World War, the Allies' intelligence community was almost nonexistent in the years leading up to 1914.

Downplaying the Importance of Spies

During the Boer War in 1899, the British had had surprisingly accurate intelligence reports from spies, who were mostly volunteers. But there was confusion about who the spies were to be accountable to, and from whom they would take orders. Because of the confusion, one British officer recommended after the war that Britain should organize a permanent intelligence department "so that in the case of [another] war, it can be expanded rapidly."[64]

However, that recommendation was ignored. Historians say that military leaders frequently tended to downplay the importance of cloak-and-dagger activity lest it take credit away from the armies themselves. "How could [a military officer] admit a battle was won because of information secretly paid for, or because of a secret coaxed out of an officer by a prostitute?" asks one historian. "He wouldn't dare. No military leader worth his stripes would have admitted that his men didn't win the battle by guts alone—it would have been tantamount to saying they cheated!"[65]

But as Europe began gearing up for war in the early 1900s, it became more and more clear that espionage was going to be necessary. Even before the fighting began, governments wanted information about what weapons were being developed or what nations were forming alliances with one another. Consequently, the governments of the Allied nations began trying to organize their intelligence-gathering capabilities.

Spy and Counterspy

Britain had a great deal of success with its new Special Intelligence Bureau, which would later be called MI5. It was headed by Sir Vernon Kell, a man with a great ability to learn languages (he could speak seven fluently). Kell was given a tiny office with two desks, two chairs, and a small cupboard.

Australian troops charge the enemy's positions. Accurate intelligence reports could be critical in determining the victor in combat.

"He was given no detailed instructions," explains one historian, "because no one was quite sure what he was supposed to do."[66] This was the state of British intelligence in 1909; by the end of World War I, however, Kell would have a staff of more than seven hundred.

Although he was given no real guidance, Kell soon realized an important function of his agency—counterintelligence. Not only was it important to recruit and monitor the activities of spies helping Britain and its allies, it was also crucial to identify and monitor foreign agents spying in Britain. In fact, Kell's first success came in an operation in 1910 involving a great number of German spies operating in Britain.

Working in tandem with a handful of British police who normally dealt with threats of Irish terrorism (tensions between Ireland and Britain were strong), Kell had become suspicious of a barber named Karl Ernst. Ernst's shop was frequented by German vacationers as well as German soldiers stationed in England. This in itself would probably not have caused Kell concern, but something else certainly did.

The Barber and the Letter Drop

When Kaiser Wilhelm came to Britain in 1910 to attend the funeral of King Edward VII, one of the men accompanying him was a captain of the German navy, known to be the head of German naval intelligence. Kell was surprised when the officer took a cab to Ernst's drab little barbershop. Investigating further, Kell and his agents found that Ernst's shop received an enormous amount of mail, mostly from seaports around the English coast.

The letters were quietly intercepted by Kell's department and found to contain information about the British fleet and Royal Navy. The shop also occasionally received packages from

Germany containing many letters with British stamps. The MI5 department realized that Ernst's shop was what those in the espionage community call a "letter drop," as one intelligence expert explains:

Sir Vernon Kell headed Britain's Special Intelligence Bureau, which later became the legendary MI5 of spy novels and movies.

German intelligence sent him packages which contained letters, bearing British postage stamps, addressed to their resident spies in England. All Ernst had to do was open the packages, post the letters and in due course forward any replies to Germany by the same means."[67]

Kell opted not to arrest the spies initially; he assumed that they would simply be replaced by other agents—and those might be harder to identify. But Kell and his MI5 agency kept an eye on them, and at the same time made sure to alter the reports slightly so that the intelligence they received was virtually useless. As soon as the war broke out, however, the spies were rounded up and jailed. During the entire war, say historians, the German secret service had no agents working in Britain.

The Challenge of Neutral Neighbors

Espionage was less difficult during World War I than it had been in other wars. The scope of the war was far larger, and neutral nations bordered warring ones. This made it easier for agents to get information. They

Hundreds of Eggs

As the war continued and it became apparent that small bits of information could make all the difference in the outcome of a battle, Allied agents were constantly on the lookout for suspicious behavior that could indicate spying. In his book *On Special Missions*, Charles Lucieto, a World War I French intelligence officer, recounts a most unusual method of communication used by a spy.

"While it is all right to have a fondness for eggs, it is not necessary to send hundreds of them to a foreign country when you are not in the poultry business."

Such were my thoughts . . . as I read a report from one of our agents in Lausanne, in which he stated that large quantities of eggs were being shipped by a man in Switzerland, of whom we were suspicious, to a certain woman who was living in France. . . . There was really nothing about her to lead us to think that she was given to spying. We knew all about what she did; there was nothing suspicious about her mail; her telephone conversations left nothing to be desired. . . . Why the deuce had she such a craving for eggs?

As I had no right to overlook even the tiniest clue, I ordered that the eggs addressed to her should be sent to my office before they were delivered. At first sight there was nothing suspicious about them. But in such matters one has to get to the bottom of things, so I sent the eggs to a laboratory where, surrounded by the greatest secrecy, our chemists were doing their bit for the welfare of the nation. . . . The next day I received the following report: "A chemical examination of the eggs . . . shows that on the shells of some of them are messages written in invisible ink. . . . The messages have to do with military operations that are now underway, but we have not yet been able to make complete translations of them."

The matter, moreover, did not stop at that. From various sources we found that other eggs were being smuggled across the border from that same place in Switzerland. Guards were stationed at various places along the border and, because of the understanding that existed between the French and Swiss customs officials, the traffic in these "literary eggs" soon stopped.

did not necessarily have to go behind enemy lines to find information; they could instead meet a contact in Belgium or Switzerland, for example.

But while a neutral government was not a threat to a spy, counterspies certainly were. Allied counterspies kept a close watch in neutral countries looking for informants who were making their way back to France after meeting a contact; there were probably an equal number of German counterspies watching for informants en route back to Germany. One former British intelligence officer later recalled that Switzerland seemed to have more spies than anywhere on earth during the war; there were "agents in the pay of every state at war [who] literally elbowed one another in the street."[68]

With so many enemy agents at hand, it was important for a spy to keep any written messages well hidden. Books, journals, and notebooks were common hiding places for messages—so much so, in fact, that most officials manning the border points at warring countries soon began confiscating all books or journals. The challenge, then, was to invent new ways to conceal the information being carried—or, for the counteragent, to discover those ways of concealing messages.

Tricks of the Trade

One early trick used by spies on both sides was to write down a few notes on a train timetable or a rolled-up newspaper. An agent could leave this message without suspicion, putting it into the padded arm of the train seat or slipping it into the mesh back of a seat, where an agent's contact would quickly retrieve it. Of course, there was always a chance that an innocent civilian might accidentally pick up a paper with important intelligence in its margin. Such occurrences were not uncommon.

Some agents preferred to keep the message on their person, even though this was far more dangerous. Agents caught with intelligence information in a pocket or sock would have a difficult time claiming it was not theirs. Police or government agents in a warring country would arrest and jail a suspected agent. Counterspies, however, were far more ruthless—often opting to kill the spy on the spot. Thus, imaginative hiding places were often a matter of life and death.

Invisible Ink

Some French agents hid messages in wooden legs, inside casts, and between gums and their false teeth. Many women wove messages in long strings into their braids or sewed them in the collar of a coat or jacket. One British agent had an unlit pipe clamped between his teeth, the tobacco resting on small bits of paper on which intelligence was written. If he felt that someone was looking suspiciously at him for any reason, he would simply light his pipe, destroying any evidence of espionage.

The use of invisible ink flourished during the First World War, and although it had been used many times in previous wars, both armies made improvements on it. Most invisible inks were made from common substances such as lemon juice, milk, or even

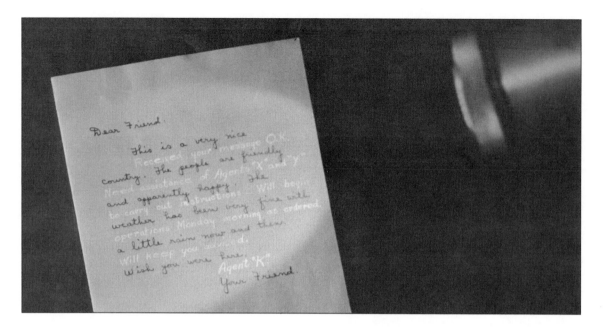

urine. Words written in such inks were invisible, but exposure to heat would turn them a brownish color.

Both armies came up with inks that were more difficult to detect, however. The Germans developed an ink that could only be read by exposing it to iodine fumes. The British came up with a red ink that was waterproof—it could get wet, yet could easily be read when activated by a hot iron or match. These inks were valuable, and couriers attempting to deliver batches of the ink to their contacts were undertaking a dangerous mission.

Counterspies were always on the lookout for supplies of the ink. A medicine bottle containing liquid was far too obvious a hiding place. To avoid being caught, a courier might soak a pair of shoelaces in invisible ink and then wear the laces until handing them

Improved invisible inks were a valuable asset to spies in the First World War.

off to a contact. Once in a safe place, the contact could pour a small amount of warm water over the laces to retrieve the ink.

Cutting Cables

While delivering batches of invisible ink and relaying carefully hidden messages utilized the talents of hundreds of spies, there were other ways that espionage was being used. In fact, one of the very first aggressive actions of the British in World War I involved the destruction of one of Germany's most valuable communication tools—its telegraph system. Germany had five large telegraph cables that lay underwater, running from Embden on the German-Dutch border, down the English Channel to Spain, France, Africa, North America, and South America.

Before dawn on August 5, 1914, the British ship *Telconia* dredged up the cables and severed them, virtually cutting Germany off from the outside world. The only other telegraph lines available to the Germans were British-owned, hardly a secure means of communication for the German military.

The recourse had to be letters, which were slow and always in danger of being intercepted, or the newest form of communication, the radio. Never before used in war, the radio—often referred to as the wireless—seemed to have great potential in warfare, for it allowed the immediate communication between army units or warships and headquarters without the need for cables or wires. However, the drawbacks to radio communication would soon become apparent.

Ciphers and Codes

Unlike the telegraph, whose wires contained the messages being transmitted, radio messages traveled on special frequencies in the open air. As a result, someone with a receiver tuned to the same frequency could eavesdrop on others' communication. Because of the ever-present danger of being overheard by enemy radio operators, armies had to use ciphers or codes when using the wireless.

Ciphers and codes are systems used to disguise the true meaning of messages so that eavesdroppers will be unable to gather intelligence. Of the two, ciphers tend to be

---

Agent Maugham

In 1915, noted British author W. Somerset Maugham was living in Switzerland. He had hoped to join the army but was rejected for three reasons: He was too short, he was too old, and he was club-footed. He became an ambulance driver for a short period of time until the newly organized British intelligence department recruited him as a spy of sorts.

Maugham was given the responsibility of keeping an eye on suspected German agents and their contacts operating in Switzerland. Intelligence personnel thought that since Maugham had extensive social contacts throughout Switzerland—as well as within the European literary community as a whole—he would have access to parties and events that German agents would likely attend.

The fact that Maugham was a famous writer who spoke fluent French and German gave him a perfect cover; however, Maugham was the first to admit he did not look the part of a spy. He wore expensive, custom-made clothes, complete with walking stick and spats. He had a pronounced stutter, and an earlier bout with tuberculosis resulted in frequent severe coughing fits.

One of Maugham's first assignments was to contact an English spy who had a German wife. The agent was suspected of having "turned"—that is, having agreed to work for the Germans while pretending to continue his work for British intelligence. Maugham not only made contact but was able to convince the agent to go to France for a literary event, where the British arrested him.

Even while working at espionage, Maugham managed to continue his writing. His novel *Ahendon* was based on his own experiences as a spy during World War I. In the foreword to the book, he wrote, "The work of an agent in the Intelligence Department is on the whole monotonous. A lot of it is uncommonly useless."

---

somewhat simpler; each letter of a word is represented by either another letter or a number. In simple ciphers, the same letter or number is always substituted for a particular letter, much like the puzzles called cryptograms. Codes are quite different. In a code, some symbol, word, or phrase is substituted for a whole word or even an entire sentence. The sender creating the message and the recipient both need a codebook, sometimes called a key, in order to understand it.

Although both codes and ciphers had been used for centuries before the First World War, never had there been so many opportunities for armies to devise codes and ciphers, as well as to attempt to crack those of the other side. By the time the war ended in 1918, the Allies would make enormous strides in both areas.

A demonstration of a cipher, a system used to disguise communications.

"More Fitted for the Playthings of Schoolboys"

The naval branch of British intelligence performed the best work in encrypting, or solving ciphers and codes. Known as Room 40—named for the room they occupied at Royal Navy headquarters—this collection of mathematicians, linguists, and cryptologists not only worked to crack German codes and ciphers but also oversaw the encoding of messages to the British navy.

Room 40's staff noticed early on that the British codes were far too simple. In a strongly worded letter to military and government leaders, Room 40 warned that the Allies would have to make some rapid progress if they wanted to keep their transmitted messages secret. They stated that "the British Fleet itself used codes and ciphers of ridiculous simplicity, more fitted for the playthings of schoolboys than for the dissemination of orders during important operations."[69]

A variety of detailed codebooks were created for the Allies—some for use by the navy, another for diplomatic use, another for use by infantry, and so on. It was also important that a code not be used for too long, for German code breakers were always working to solve Allied codes. Given enough time, they would crack a code, and important secrets might be lost.

One American intelligence expert recalls that three or four weeks would be the

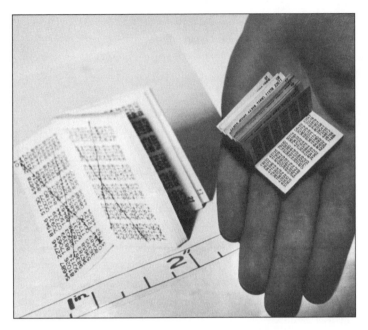

A variety of codebooks such as this miniaturized one were created for the Allies. To maintain security, the codes were changed frequently.

longest the Allies would go before installing new code systems:

> After that the enemy would have solved it, anyway. A trusty ruse was to order by radio an "attack" in a sector where already we had withdrawn our troops from the front line—then watch for the German barrage to come down on that section. If it did, we changed our code."[70]

Gaining Access to Germany's Codes

Because codebooks contained the keys to deciphering important messages, they were supposed to be guarded with one's life. If they fell into enemy hands, important messages could be decoded and all attempts at secrecy would fail. Hundreds of lives—sometimes thousands—might depend on keeping the codebook safe.

Three events early in the war gave British intelligence an edge. The first occurred when a Russian cruiser sank a German vessel in the Gulf of Finland. Russian sailors surveying the debris noticed a dead German sailor whose clamped hands clutched the German naval codebook. The cruiser captain notified Britain, and soon the book was in the hands of the delighted cryptographers at Room 40, who were able to decode all messages to and from German ships for several weeks.

Two other incidents produced codebooks. A British trawler retrieved from a sunken German U-boat a chest that contained a different codebook—this one for naval attachés. And finally, a diplomatic codebook was left behind by one German consul in Persia (now Iran) when the arrival of British troops forced him to flee suddenly. These books, too, provided Room 40 with a wealth of information about how German intelligence encrypted their messages.

But knowledge of what an enemy army or navy was planning to do often presented a difficult choice. If Room 40 decoded a message giving the exact location of Germany's U-boats, British officials had to decide whether to dispatch their fleets to those locations—thereby alerting the Germans that their codes had been cracked—or simply keep listening to the messages and thereby allow the U-boats to sink more Allied ships.

This kind of choice came up time and time again during the war, but never did it pose such a thorny problem as when the British intercepted a telegram sent from Germany to Mexico. The consequences, especially for the United States, were gigantic, for the message it contained would drag America into the war.

The Zimmermann Telegram

On Wednesday morning, January 17, 1917, a stack of papers—the sum total of the past night's communication—was in Room 40 waiting to be decoded. One message, a telegram from the German foreign minister Arthur Zimmermann to the German ambassador in Mexico, contained a bombshell.

In the telegram, Zimmermann informed the ambassador of Germany's plan to resume unrestricted submarine warfare. In addition, Zimmermann hoped the United States would stay neutral; if it did not, however, Germany was proposing an alliance with Mexico, who would reclaim its lost territories of Texas, Arizona, and New Mexico.

The head of Room 40, Rear Admiral Reginald "Blinker" Hall, knew that when the United States learned of the telegram, there would be great public outcry against Germany, and America would enter the war. But Hall was nervous. Although Britain and the Allies wanted to have the United States join them in the war, Hall did not want Germany to know that they had the capacity to crack its codes (the codebook left behind by the Persian ambassador was used to read the Zimmermann telegram). Somehow, writes one historian, "the German goose must be kept alive to go on laying its golden eggs."[71]

Hall deftly sidestepped the problem, although he had to wait for almost three weeks to do it. He instructed a British agent in Mexico to steal a copy of the Zimmermann telegram from the German ambassador there. The agent then managed to get the telegram into American hands without causing Germany to suspect Room 40's consistent decoding of its messages. President Wilson was horrified at the telegram's contents and soon urged Congress to declare war on Germany.

Americans Way Behind

If Room 40 had once been nervous about the British being far behind in the making of codes, they must certainly have been appalled at the state of American intelligence when the United States finally entered the war. It was, in fact, almost nonexistent. In April 1917, the American Military Intelligence (MI) Office in Washington, D.C., consisted of two officers and a part-time clerk. Its yearly budget was $11,000.

Part of the reason the United States lagged so far behind the nations of Europe was that American leaders had not been preparing for war. In 1914, as France, Britain, Germany, and other nations were busily creating intelligence departments and staffs of code breakers, the new U.S.

The Zimmermann Telegram

What appeared as a Western Union telegram consisting of long columns of four- and five-digit numbers, the Zimmermann telegram, when translated, contained a stunning message from Germany to Mexico. The decoded telegram, contained in Jay Robert Nash's *Spies: A Narrative Encyclopedia of Dirty Deeds and Double Dealing from Biblical Times to Today*, is shown here in its entirety.

> Foreign Office Telegraphs January 16: Number 1, Strictly Secret. Yourself to Decipher.

> We intend to begin unrestricted U-boat warfare on the first of February. We shall endeavor in spite of this to keep the United States neutral. In the event of this not succeeding, we offer Mexico an alliance on the following basis: Make war together, make peace together. Generous financial support

and an understanding on our part that Mexico is to reconquer the lost territories in Texas, New Mexico, and Arizona. The settlement in detail is left to you.

> You will inform the President [of Mexico] of the above in the strictest secrecy as soon as the outbreak of war with the United States is certain and add the suggestion that he should, on his own initiative, invite Japan to join immediately and at the same time mediate between Japan and ourselves.

> Please call the President's attention to the fact that the ruthless employment of our submarines now offers the prospect of compelling England to make peace within a few months.

> Acknowledge receipt.
> Zimmermann.

War Bureau was just beginning to put its first real codebook together. The staff at the War Bureau understood so little about secrecy, in fact, that after they decided on a code, they sent it to a local Washington shop to be printed—unaware that something of that nature needed far more security.

A young army colonel named Ralph Van Deman realized how far the United States needed to go merely to catch up to other nations, and he singlehandedly urged the government to set up a separate intelligence service. Within forty-eight hours of pleading his case before members of the War Department, Van Deman had not only gotten the intelligence service, he'd been made the head of the MI office. He immediately got to work recruiting the most talented people he could find.

Herbert Yardley

The most interesting of the new recruits was a brilliant young telegraph clerk named Herbert Yardley. Working in the State Department, Yardley occasionally amused himself by solving coded or ciphered messages that came in for President Wilson— doing most of them effortlessly. Just as Room 40 had criticized British codes, Yardley continually told his superiors in the telegraph office that the government's codes were almost embarrassingly easy to crack, but no one took him seriously.

Yardley finally decided to prove what he'd claimed and quickly deciphered what the U.S. government officials believed to be a highly coded letter to President Wilson

from the American ambassador in Berlin. "He then pointed out to his superiors," writes one historian, "that the British, then controllers of the Atlantic Cable, could obviously do the same and were privy to all of America's most secret diplomatic messages."[72]

Yardley was immediately assigned to head a new department in American intelligence called MI8 (Military Intelligence, Section 8). Within only a few months, Yardley and his staff had broken a number of the most secret German codes, including one used in a letter found on a German agent that implicated the agent in two acts of sabotage on American soil.

Control of the Atlantic Cable provided Britain with access to America's most secret diplomatic messages.

Choctaw Code-Talkers

Yardley was responsible for a great deal of growth in American codes and intelligence. However, there was one brilliant strategy in American secret communication that he had nothing to do with—the use of the Native American Choctaw language as a code. Choctaw, spoken by the Choctaw Indians, was seized upon by a desperate American commander during the final German push of the war.

An American battalion, which included eight Choctaw, had important information they needed to communicate to headquarters. However, the Germans had recently broken the Americans' infantry codes, so the

Choctaw soldiers take aim with their sidearms. One American battalion used eight Choctaw soldiers to encode and send vital messages to its headquarters.

battalion was in trouble. All hope for secure communication seemed lost until the commander overheard two of his men talking in their native language. After the commander learned from the two men that there were six others who could speak Choctaw, including two more at headquarters, he was jubilant. He asked one of the men to send the important message in Choctaw to headquarters, to another native speaker.

The experiment worked perfectly, and, as it turned out, there could not have been a better language than Choctaw for encoding a vital message. There were twenty-six dialects of the language, only two of which had ever been written down. And since the number of native speakers of Choctaw was diminishing even in the United States, the chances of a German who could understand any of it were almost zero.

The messages to be communicated often needed words that did not exist in Choctaw. To improvise, explains one Choctaw historian, "'little gun shoot fast' was substituted for machine gun, and the battalions were indicated by one, two or three grains of corn."[73]

Using Choctaw in codes was a lifesaver to that battalion in the closing months of World War I. The eight Choctaw speakers were very busy during that time, handling a great deal of the communication between various army stations. Not one message sent in Choctaw was ever intercepted and decoded, another important stride in espionage accomplished during the Great War.

Chapter 6

The Intangible Weapon

Just as the First World War brought major new developments in a wide variety of weaponry, it also marked the first use of the term *total war*. The term meant that all parts of a nation were involved in fighting the war, not just the men in uniform. Farmers, munitions workers, textile workers—all were crucial parts of the war effort. "Civilians mattered in war," explain historians Jay Winter and Blaine Baggett, "because it was their weapons which were wielded by men at the front, and it was their well-being for which the soldiers were fighting in the first place."[74]

Morale Was Vital

But the military and political leaders of both sides knew that it was not enough for civilians merely to produce weapons and supplies or grow food for their soldiers. It was important for them to be supportive of the war effort as well. After all, as months dragged into years, the cost of the war grew to be staggering, in terms of both money and lives spent. If citizens became critical of the war or were reluctant to send their sons and husbands to the front, all would be lost.

Morale on the home front was vital for winning the war. To keep enthusiasm and support strong, both sides used propaganda, or various means of persuading people to believe certain things or behave in certain ways. No matter what means were used, however, the goal was the same: to provide a steady supply of soldiers at the front and at the same time keep civilians enthusiastic about winning the war, no matter how long it took. Propaganda was not always a tangible weapon, but it was one of the most powerful of the war.

One common theme of Allied propaganda was that young men should enlist in the army. Colorful posters—more than 200,000 in Britain alone—appeared in every shop window and on every public building. Some used peer pressure; one showed laughing young men in jaunty uniforms with flags flying behind them as they

Propaganda posters were used to provide a steady supply of soldiers at the front.

invited other young men to become one of their number. Another used guilt; it showed two pictures of the same young man, one in uniform and the other sitting in a chair reading, a tennis racket leaning against the chair. The poster asked any young man viewing it which picture his father would show to friends.

White Feathers

The fear of looking cowardly—especially in front of a wife or girlfriend—was a powerful motivator, too. In 1914, a British admiral founded the Order of the White Feather, based on the idea that a white feather symbolized cowardice. The order employed young women to give out white feathers to any young men they encountered who had not joined the army.

Many British men who had decided not to enlist reconsidered when faced with a white feather. The shame of being accused of cowardice in public, they believed, was far worse than being sent to the front. James Lovegrove remembers being accosted by members of the Order of the White Feather on his way to work one morning when he was barely sixteen:

> They started shouting and yelling at me, calling me all sorts of names for not being a soldier! Do you know what they did? They stuck a white feather in my coat, meaning I was a coward. Oh, I did feel dreadful, so ashamed. I went to the recruiting office. The sergeant there couldn't stop laughing at me, saying things like, "Looking for your father, sonny?" and "Come back next year when the war's over!"[75]

Targeting America

A great deal of Allied propaganda targeted neutral nations, especially the United States. Because France had been invaded, its government did not need to appeal to its citizens to enlist. However, the French generated a great deal of propaganda aimed at bringing the United States into the war.

Colorful posters showed entwined French and American flags, and many reminded Americans how the Frenchman the Marquis de Lafayette had assisted America during the Revolutionary War.

British propagandists applied pressure to the United States, too. By 1917, the German U-boats had been successful in limiting the food and supplies going to Britain; half a ton of British supplies were being sunk each month. Though the food supply was not as dire as it was in Germany, British civilians faced shortages in coal, sugar, potatoes, and other staples. Without an infusion of American troops and supplies, the war would be lost, and Britain knew it.

Sir Gilbert Parker was put in charge of British propaganda in the United States, and he made certain that the Allied point of view in the war was strongly presented. Hundreds of journals and newspapers were sent each week to the United States. British essayists would describe the war using

The Marquis de Lafayette (left) confers with General George Washington during the American Revolutionary War. Some propaganda posters reminded Americans how the French had assisted America during this conflict.

phrases they knew would resonate with American readers. "This is not a war of peoples," one wrote, "but of despots and diplomatists. It is, we may hope, the last supreme struggle of the old dispensation against the old." Another wrote, "Every sword that is drawn against Germany is a sword drawn for peace. . . . The victory of Germany will mean the permanent enthronement of the War God over all human affairs."[76]

A Difficult Challenge

However, as powerful as such pro-Allied material was, the propaganda of France and Britain was not responsible for the United States finally entering the war. The Zimmermann telegram and the sinking of American ships by German U-boats were the factors that led to President Woodrow Wilson's decision.

But Wilson and his advisers knew it would be a very difficult challenge to whip up enthusiasm for this war among the American people. The United States had not been attacked or invaded, as France had. Bomb-laden zeppelins were not gliding over their cities, as they were in Britain. When Wilson asked Congress for a declaration of war on April 2, 1917, he was departing from his promise to keep America at peace, a promise that had greatly helped him win a second term. Although there were many Americans who were eager to join the fighting in Europe, most Americans were not interested in going to war.

Another thing that made it difficult to sell the idea of war was the varied backgrounds of the American people. The United States was a nation of immigrants. In fact, in 1917, one-third of the population were immigrants. Eight million were German Americans, and many of them were sympathetic to the cause of their homeland.

Even if the majority of the population had been interested in fighting, the United States was simply not ready for war. With a woefully small and untested army, the United States would need to add more than 1 million men within a few weeks, and this would be a problem. Americans were notoriously uncooperative when forced to do anything, especially something as dramatic as joining the army. The last time the U.S. government had attempted to force enlistment was during the Civil War, and more than one thousand people died in the riots that ensued.

In entering World War I, the American people would be participating in total war, just as the Allied civilians were. And like the governments of Britain, France, and Russia, the United States would need to make sure that its citizens were enthusiastic and supportive of the war and all the challenges and difficulties it would bring.

The Committee on Public Information

To accomplish this seemingly impossible task, Wilson set up the Committee on Public Information (CPI). Its job would be to promote the war to the American people using various types of propaganda. The CPI borrowed some ideas from successful

A draft riot erupts during the Civil War. Avoiding such conflicts during World War I was a difficult challenge for the United States.

Allied propaganda, such as the artistic, inspirational posters that urged young men to enlist. Other types of propaganda were originals created by the committee.

The leader of the CPI was a former journalist named George Creel, a longtime Wilson supporter. To help the CPI get its message out, Creel recruited well-known talents from business, the press, the academic world, art and design, and the film industry. "It was a gargantuan advertising agency," recalled one historian, "the likes of which the country had never known."[77]

Creel and his associates believed that in times of peace, it was permissible for people to hold different opinions about politics and world affairs. However, during war such differences were potentially dangerous, causing rifts where there should be unity. During wartime, wrote one propaganda expert,

It is no longer possible to fuse the waywardness of individuals in the furnace of the war dance; a new and subtler instrument must weld thousands and even millions of human beings into one amalgamated mass of hate and will and hope. A new flame must burn out the canker of dissent and temper the steel of bellicose enthusiasm. The name of this new hammer and anvil of social solidarity is propaganda.[78]

Hollywood Goes to War

Creel organized the CPI into nineteen subdivisions that would each focus on a certain aspect of propaganda during the war. For example, the Industrial Relations Department devoted itself to selling the war to the workers and labor unions. The Picture Publicity Department, under the leadership of famed artist Charles Dana Gibson, turned out hundreds of different designs for posters reminding people to support the war.

The Division of Films encouraged Hollywood to produce movies that would make people proud of their fighting men and proud to be Americans. This division also ensured that the war was heavily promoted in movies made and shown in the United States. Hollywood producers and directors were happy to comply, for none wished to appear unpatriotic.

Between 1917 and 1919, movies with such titles as *To Hell with the Kaiser* and *Pershing's Crusaders* became big favorites with American audiences. One film, *The Kaiser: Beast of Berlin*, elicited an enthusiastic response from an Omaha, Nebraska, newspaper:

Fourteen thousand people—the largest number that ever saw a motion picture

Pictured is a poster for a movie produced by the Committee on Public Information.

in Omaha in one week—saw *The Kaiser* at the Auditorium in that city last week. Eight hundred children attended a "kid matinee" on Saturday afternoon and the sixteen-piece orchestra that furnished the music could not be heard above the din they made. . . . Wild cheering marked every show when the young captain socked the Kaiser on the jaw.[79]

The Four Minute Men

Another of Creel's innovations was a group of speakers known as the Four Minute Men. They were used to get the war message out to large groups of people before the age of radio and television. The men went into communities and found a suitable spot to stir up excitement and enthusiasm about the war in four minutes or less. Since Creel's statistics indicated that each day between 10 and 13 million Americans went to the movies, many Four Minute Men gave their speeches immediately after the show.

They spoke on a variety of topics—from "There Are German Spies in Our Midst" and "Why You Should Buy Liberty Bonds" to "Why Johnny Should Enlist" and "Children Must Learn the American Way." To help the men become as effective as possible, the CPI published bulletins with tips such as "Be natural and direct. Sincerity wears no frills," and "You represent the United States of America. Don't forget it, and don't give your audience occasion to forget it."[80]

The Four Minute Men proved to be wildly popular wherever they went. It was one of the CPI's most successful programs.

"It's Duty, Boy"

One of the topics the Four Minute Men spoke about was the sacrifice parents made to send a son off to war. Occasionally, instead of making a speech, they would read a poem written by CPI staffers. The following poem, included in Alfred Cornebise's *War as Advertised: The Four Minute Men and America's Crusade 1917–1918*, makes it clear how parents should feel about "slackers."

It's Duty, Boy
My boy must never bring disgrace to his
   immortal sires—
At Valley Forge and Lexington they kindled
   freedom's fires,
John's father died at Gettysburg, mine fell
   at Chancellorsville;
While John himself was with the boys who
   charged up San Juan Hill.
And John, if he was living now, would
   surely say with me,
"No son of ours shall e'er disgrace our
   grand old family tree
By turning out a slacker when his country
   needs his aid."
It is not of such timber that America was
   made.

I'd rather you had died at birth or not
   been born at all,
Than know that I had raised a son who
   cannot hear the call
That freedom has sent round the world, its
   precious rights to save—
This call is meant for you, my boy, and I
   would have you brave;
And though my heart is breaking, boy, I
   bid you do your part,
And show the world no son of mine is
   cursed with craven heart;
And if, perchance, you ne'er return, my
   later days to cheer,
And I have only memories of my brave
   boy, so dear,
I'd rather have it so, my boy, and know
   you bravely died
Than have a living coward sit supinely by
   my side.
To save the world from sin, my boy, God
   gave his only son—
He's asking for MY boy, today, and may
   His will be done.

Creel was extremely proud of his legions of speakers, a force that grew from fifteen hundred men in 1917 to seventy-five thousand men by the war's end. Said Creel, "The idea, from the very first, had the sweep of a prairie fire."[81] Theater owners reported that they sold far more movie tickets when people knew there would be a short speech afterward; many citizens expressed their wish that politicians would also limit their speeches to four minutes.

Deciding

The CPI was very definite about what was appropriate or inappropriate, not only in the speeches Americans heard but also in the films they watched. For instance, films that stressed compromise or pacifism or movies that showed any of the Allies in a poor light did not receive the CPI's recommendation seal. One film about the American Revolution was refused by CPI officials because it made the British army seem mean-spirited.

What the CPI did for film, it did for America's reading material as well. The Division of News was a crucial part of the CPI; it acted as a filter for all the war information that was communicated to the public. Rather than have many different versions or interpretations of the same story, CPI staffers would write up press releases and send them to newspapers. From this news, the newspapers could write their stories.

The reasoning behind this, explained Creel, was that if unchecked, newspapers might inadvertently give out sensitive information to Germany. Mentioning a ship's name in a story, or even naming a place where a battle or confrontation took place might help the enemy defeat the Allies if a German spy read the newspaper account. Such carelessness in the press, Creel said, was bad enough during peacetime, "but is a positive menace when the nation is at war."[82]

Demonizing the Germans

Another way of controlling the information civilians received was in the purposeful demonizing of the German army. (The German propagandists no doubt did the same for the Allies.) Demonization of the enemy is a tried-and-true part of propaganda; it is far easier to whip up hatred toward "a murdering horde," for example, than toward "another country's army." Hate, observed author Arthur Conan Doyle, "has its uses in war. . . . It steels the mind and sets the resolution as no other emotion can do."[83]

Although propagandists in the United States were not the only ones to demonize the Germans, many historians feel that CPI pamphlets, posters, and even some of the Four Minute Men's speeches went further than most. In some posters, for example, German soldiers are portrayed as almost subhuman, with hulking walks and slobbering mouths. They carry knives and swords dripping blood as they walk down American streets. In one poster, a German soldier is holding a bayonet on which several small children are impaled. In another, a smirking German soldier is pulling a small, frightened girl by the hand.

The word *Hun* was frequently used in such propaganda, as it was in British and French propaganda. Huns were an especially ruthless and warlike people who lived around A.D. 400 in what is now Germany. By using the term in reference to modern Germans, the Allies were equating the two peoples.

Atrocities

But nothing stirred hate in Allied civilians as much as the atrocity stories that propagandists circulated. Most were untrue, but that didn't matter. A story of German soldiers raping and killing women, for example, or handing out poison candy to small children in Belgium accomplished a number of things.

As a result of the atrocity stories, more young men enlisted in the army, perhaps thinking that they could pay the Germans back for such behavior. More civilians bought war bonds, too, thereby helping the

A German soldier terrorizes a woman in a movie. Hollywood films demonized Germans in order to build hatred for the enemy.

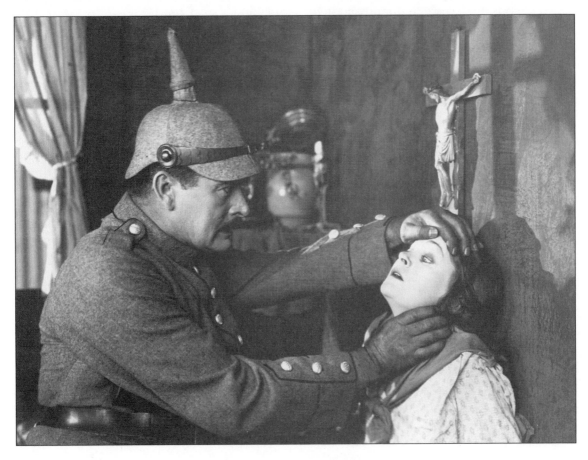

government with the expense of the war. The sacrifices that citizens were making—the rationing of certain foods, for example—seemed less painful. If spending money on war bonds or eating less meat would help their boys win the war and stop the German cruelty, it was worth it.

The stories themselves were horrifying. Many of the atrocities described by the Russians involved the mutilation of prisoners. Tales of the shooting of Belgian children (made all the more horrible because of Belgium's neutral status) abounded among the Allied nations. One story frequently quoted by CPI workers was about the shootings of Red Cross workers by German soldiers.

One of the most gruesome stories that circulated among all the Allied nations was about German soap factories. In April 1917, a British newspaper reporter made up a story that the Germans were melting down the corpses of Allied soldiers to extract glycerine for soap. The story ran next to a photograph of dead bodies awaiting burial. Interestingly, historians say that this piece of propaganda came back to haunt the Allies a generation later. When the Germans *did* commit atrocities during World War II against Jews, Poles, and others—including making soap from corpses—few were willing to believe it, assuming it to be more of the same propaganda.

A Nurse's Tragedy

Many atrocity stories circulated among the Allied nations. The story of the British nurse mutilated by a German soldier was one of the first. It was discovered some time later that the nurse's sister had made up the story. The newspaper article that first reported the story is included in Arthur Ponsonby's *Falsehood in War-Time: Containing an Assortment of Lies Circulated Throughout the Nations During the Great War.*

"A Nurse's Tragedy"

News has reached Dumfries of the shocking death of a Dumfries young woman, Nurse Grace Hume, who went out to Belgium at the outbreak of the war. Nurse Hume was engaged at the camp hospital at Vilvorde, and she was the victim of horrible cruelty at the hands of German soldiers. Her breasts were cut off and she died in great agony.

Nurse Hume's family received a note written shortly before she died. It was dated September 6th, and ran: "Dear Kate, This is to say goodbye. Have not long to live. Hospital has been set on fire. Germans cruel. A man here had his head cut off. My right breast has been taken away. Give my love to———. Goodbye. GRACE."

Nurse Hume's left breast was cut away after she had written the note. She was a young woman of twenty-three and was formerly a nurse in Huddersfield Hospital.

Nurse Mullard, of Inverness, delivered the note personally to Nurse Hume's sister at Dumfries. She was also at Vilvorde, and she states that Nurse Hume acted the part of a heroine. A German attacked a wounded soldier whom Nurse Hume was taking to hospital. The nurse took his gun and shot the German dead.

"The Star," September 16, 1914.

The German Threat at Home

There is no question that the CPI's propaganda increased many Americans' support of the war effort. However, the atrocity stories and the demonization of the German army had some dangerous consequences within the United States. Anti-German sentiments were aimed not only at the army that the Allies were fighting in Europe but at the millions of German Americans who lived in the United States.

Some leaders spoke out about the dangers of what they called "hyphenated Americans." President Wilson himself, in a speech to Congress, worried about the true nature of some of the foreign-born, calling them "creatures of passion, disloyalty, and anarchy." Another government official warned that "the melting pot has not melted" and that "there are vast communities in the Nation thinking today not in terms of America, but in terms of Old World prejudices, theories, and animosities."[84]

Such thinking translated quickly into a frenzy of distrust—and it was exhibited in hundreds of ways. Some were silly, such as the renaming of German things with American-sounding names. Dachshunds became "Liberty hounds." German measles became "Liberty Measles." A hamburger (named after a city in Germany) was renamed a "Liberty Sandwich."

Intolerance and Mob Violence

Some things that changed, however, were not silly. For example, high school and college German classes were banned in many school districts. Others, hesitant to ban the classes altogether, agreed to cut in half the number of credits awarded for taking German. In Iowa, the governor made it illegal to speak German on the telephone, on streetcars, and in any public place in the state. This made life miserable for many German Americans whose English was poor and thus spoke German with other German American friends and family.

The heightened suspicion and hate sometimes led to violence. In a small town in Illinois, a mob seized a young German American coal miner named Robert Prager. Stripped, wrapped with an American flag, and dragged barefoot down Main Street, Prager was lynched as five hundred townspeople cheered. After finding the mob members not guilty, one jurist shouted, "Well, I guess nobody can say we aren't loyal now."[85]

The intolerance was not limited to the German Americans. Many groups were singled out for suspicion, including pacifists and others who raised objections to the war. Some had their houses painted yellow (the color of cowardice); others were tarred and feathered.

The fear of German Americans and pacifists in their midst caused mild hysteria in many communities. Unfortunately, some of the voices that could have been most calming actually ignited more intolerance. Many teachers, professors, and even clergy were eager to show their patriotism by denouncing German Americans and pacifists. For instance, one pastor in New Jersey praised a group of factory workers, known as the Rail Committee, who came up with what he thought was a wonderful way of dealing with any fellow worker who did not support the war 100 percent:

> In a yard at Seattle, the Rail Committee has an iron pipe which is called the Liberty Rail. . . . When a workman utters a disloyal sentiment, fails to buy bonds or war-saving stamps, or in other ways proves that he is lukewarm, the Rail Committee waits on him. The Liberty rail is heated at the forge, and the disloyal workman is ridden about the yards on the hot rail. At one time, I was told,

This man has been tarred and feathered. American propaganda at times heightened suspicion and led to hate crimes like these.

there were twelve men in a Seattle hospital recovering from Liberty Rail rides.[86]

While these excessses were definitely not part of George Creel's Committee on Public Information, they were nevertheless a measure of how well the war was "sold" to American citizens in 1917. Even though the American people had reelected President Wilson on his campaign promise to keep America out of war, they quickly responded to CPI techniques.

The Legacy of the War's Weapons

In the hands of skilled people like Geoge Creel, propaganda had become a powerful weapon during the First World War. Because this war was so different from wars before it, it was more important than ever to win the support and enthusiasm of civilians. This had been done before, but never as powerfully as in World War I.

Just as the war's propaganda techniques achieved both positive and negative results, other weapons of World War I achieved a wide range of success too. Familiar weapons reached their full potential. The machine gun almost single-handedly forced both armies to set aside their plans for an offensive war. Submarines caused enormous losses that resulted in huge shortages of food, fuel, and supplies for Britain; historians maintain that if Germany had not backed off its unrestricted warfare at sea, Britain most assuredly would have had to surrender. Espionage also grew into matu-